G102.

THE DEEP THINGS OF GOD

THE DEEP THINGS
OF GOD

by

NORMAN P. GRUBB

LUTTERWORTH PRESS

LONDON

First published 1958

COPYRIGHT © 1958 NORMAN P. GRUBB

Printed in Great Britain by Butler & Tanner Ltd., Frome and London

CONTENTS

1. WHY THIS BOOK?   7
2. THE KEY TO THE MEANING OF LIFE   9
3. THE ORIGIN OF EVIL   12
4. RESTORATION IN ITS FIRST STAGE   17
5. MAN'S BASIC FACULTY   21
6. WHAT REALLY HAPPENS AT REGENERATION?   24
7. THE ROOT IS DEALT WITH   28
8. WHAT REALLY IS THE NEW MAN?   34
9. THE PROBLEM OF DUALITY—GOOD AND EVIL   38
10. SELF-CONSCIOUSNESS AND
        CHRIST-CONSCIOUSNESS   43
11. THE MEANING OF THE LAW IN SCRIPTURE   48
12. THE MARRIAGE OF LAW AND GRACE   56
13. THE BELIEVER AND ROMANS 7   63
14. FALSE CONDEMNATION   66
15. FAITH IN ACTION   70
16. THE GIFTS OF THE SPIRIT   76
17. THE DIALECTICAL PRINCIPLE IN ALL LIFE   84
18. IMPERFECTION POINTS TO PERFECTION   93
19. HOW TO TURN EVIL INTO GOOD   98
20. NEED IS THE EVIDENCE OF SUPPLY   103
21. TRUE ECUMENICITY   108
22. LOVE IN ACTION   115

1   WHY THIS BOOK?

Through thirty-five years as a missionary in Africa and Missionary Secretary at the home base, I have been increasingly concerned with one great question: What is the Gospel in its fulness? Do I know it? Do I live it? Can I transmit it? Many hundreds of hours have I spent searching the Scriptures and absorbing the writings of those who have asked and answered the same questions; many hundreds of times have I spoken on this subject, and each talk, with the exercise of mind and heart in preparation and delivery, has pushed the preacher a little further into his own message: I have also attempted four times to put what I had learned into print—in two books, *The Law of Faith* and *The Liberating Secret*, and in two brochures, *Touching the Invisible* and *Continuous Revival*.

The most recent of these, *The Liberating Secret*, put what for me was the essence of truth, as I saw it up to that time. But I am glad that Paul said it was legitimate to repeat: "to write the same things to you, to me is not grievous, but for you it is safe"! We must progress or atrophy, and the progression I have now made is to underline with the thickest possible line the main emphases of that book; but at the same time I want to bring some points into yet sharper focus, and in this shorter book to tie the main threads a bit tighter and more compactly together. So readers of *The Liberating Secret* must not mind if they recognize some of the same message in different words.

I wish I had the teacher's gifts of compressing what he wants to say into separate and easily grasped paragraphs, also of good illustrations. I haven't either: but I want to make this attempt to outline these "mysteries" of the Spirit, which burn in me, in a shortened form, and hope that it may open windows to some into "heavenly things".

2 THE KEY TO THE MEANING OF LIFE

WE start at the fountain-head. There is only one
Person in the end—God Himself, Father, Son
and Holy Spirit. All came from Him. All returns to Him. His one and only Word, the first and final
expression of Himself, is still Himself—God the Son, who
is in the bosom of the Father. In Him is the beginning,
"the first born of all creation". In Him is the church
which is His body. In Him is the end, "that He might
gather together in one all things in Christ", Alpha and
Omega. He *is* Life. He *is* light. He *is* love. He *is* the
wisdom and power of God.

Does this sound mere theology? No, it is the key to the
meaning of life, and to the great delusion which we mis-
takenly call life. For the first essential truth for us to grasp
is that no created being has *the* life in himself. Creatures
are created to *contain* the life, not to be it in themselves:
the essence of idolatry is to claim to be what only God is.
God is God, and there are no gods beside Him. God can
never give His own godhead to another, His own nature,
His own attributes. That would be making other gods.
What God has done in the beauty and wonder of His
creation is to make creatures of infinite variety which each
in their own measure can contain God in them, and
manifest His glory. Containers are not the thing in itself.
The cup is useful, and needs to be clean, but it is not the

9

same as the water it contains. The electric bulb is needful likewise, but it is not the light that shines through it.

All creatures are on the receiving end of life. It is the one simple faculty all exercise. They *receive* air and sunlight and rain and food; and as a consequence of their receiving we who have eyes to see are ravished by *the glory of God* in the beauty of the flowers and the song of the birds, the form and colour of wing and leaf.

Man, the crown of His creation, is exactly the same. He is created a recipient. The miracle of his creation, both in its exaltedness and responsibility, is that he is made like God Himself in his faculties; but not in his attributes. He is a thinking, feeling, willing being, a spirit, clothed in soul and body. In that sense he is like God, made in the image of God. *But* he is not God. The true life, light, love, wisdom, power, meekness, humility, selflessness, holiness, is God Himself and none other. These attributes, these characteristics He could never give to another as though they were their own possessions, for that would make them gods. But just as the vegetable and animal creation live by what they receive from God in the natural realm, so man can live this other quality of life, eternal life, God's type of life, only by receiving God to live His life in him. In the marvel of His creation man can freely, intelligently, delightedly *contain* the living God, so that God lives His own divine life out through the living agency and co-operation of a human personality; but the human being never advances one iota beyond being a mere container of God for time and eternity. Never is there, nor will there be, one atom of godliness, wisdom, love, eternal life, divine power which he can call his own, so that he could say *I* am holy, *I* am wise, *I* am mighty. That is the deadly sin of all history—idolatry.

This does not mean that God's creatures on every level

have not their own capacity for action, and are created to act. They have. But even in its highest form, in humanity, the creature can never rise above self-activity. The human self is compounded of three elemental forces: contraction (drawing to oneself, covetousness), expansion (moving out from oneself, creativeness), and rotation (the consequent whirling wheel of restless selfhood, resulting from the tug-of-war of these two equal but contrary forces). The heavenly life, the life that God lives, the life of perfect love, which stills the human tempest and unites the war-ring elements, is from without, not within, the created self. It is of an "infinite qualitative distinction". The human created personality can only find its meaning, and slip into gear, when it is immersed in the Divine—His Spirit in our spirit; His mind, His will, His feelings expressed through the powers of our soul; His actions through our body: then only is the human self released from itself in spirit, soul and body to manifest the fulness of the Divine Self, the wisdom, the power, the beauty of Him who is Love. For real life, eternal life, is love—self-giving, others-serving, self-ignoring love: and that love alone is wisdom, light, power: and God alone is that love. God's power is love-power. *That* is the unique eternal life of God, and that is something completely other than the self-seeking selfhood of the creature. In that sense, the creature is the nothing, and He the all: and the human self is for ever a container, a co-operator, a manifestor, but never the One in Himself.

3   THE ORIGIN OF EVIL

Go back to the beginning, and we find that the Scripture reveals the rejection of this relationship to be original sin. Twice the prophets had unveiled to them a backward glimpse at the original anti-Christ (Is. 14: 12–14; Ezek. 28: 11–19), even as they had so many forward glimpses of the coming Christ. And both times original sin is seen to be independent selfhood. "I will be like the most High," said Lucifer. Egoism, self-centredness, self-seeking, self-sufficiency, is original sin. All other sins are mere expressions, manifestations of this original sin. A creature who in all his exaltedness as a seraph could never, never be more than a container, would make himself the thing-in-itself (the Person-in-Himself). The nothing would be something. Man would be God. That is why pride is the first of all sins. It *is* sin.

There is only one difference between the sin of Lucifer and the sin of Adam and Eve, a difference indeed of quantity, not of quality, but still very important. Lucifer went all the way in the sin of egoism. He set his will to displace God with man, the Creator-self with the created-self, the selfless-self with the selfish-self; and thus he opened the kingdom of the self-in-reverse, the kingdom of God's No, the kingdom of darkness, devil and hell. It is still God's kingdom, and we shall see the significance of that later, but it is the kingdom of God's wrath; he is still

God's devil, but an angel of God's hell instead of God's heaven. Everything is in reverse to him; evil is good to him, and good evil; he loves what should be hated and hates what should be loved. God, who is the eternal Yes to all goodness, love, mercy, and selflessness, is equally the eternal No to their opposites. If He loves the one, He equally hates the other; if He blesses the one, He equally curses the other; for it is the nature of things that to say yes to one point of view is equally to say no to its opposite. So Lucifer, the first egoist, with his hosts, who was the first to enter the forbidden realm of selfish selfhood, of self-filled rather than self-emptied selfhood, of independence rather than dependence, and thus became the spirit of sin, the essence of sin, found Himself in God's darkness, hate, anger, consuming fire.

Eve, on the other hand, was deceived (1 Tim. 2: 14) by the Tempter and listened to his lies about God, not because she consciously opposed God, but because she was tricked into thinking that to disobey God would be to her advantage. Adam sinned deliberately (1 Tim. 2: 14), but again, not so much in direct antagonism against God as under fleshly bondage to his wife. Both were more concerned with satisfying their fleshly lusts than with rebellion against God. They wanted the best of both worlds. They had not sinned that unforgivable sin against the Holy Ghost, the "wilful" sin which "tramples under foot the Son of God". Theirs was the sin of flesh rather than spirit, Satan of spirit more than flesh. As a consequence, though now children of the devil, infected with his spirit (Eph. 2: 2), partaking of his rebellious nature, walking according to the course of this world, fulfilling the desires of the flesh and the mind, they were still conscious of right as right; they had eaten of the tree of knowledge of *good* and evil; the thunders of God's law could still reverberate in their souls, of which God's word of judgment and mercy to them immediately after their disobedience is evidence. Fallen, separated from God, dead in trespasses and sins, but not yet unredeemable, as are devils: on the devil's road, under his control, but not finally fixed as devils. And that is why this is a groaning world. Bound by sin, sold under our lusts, slaves to egoism, yet ever conscious of what we ought to be; challenged by highest ideals in personal, social and political life, yet never attaining them; and constantly pointing the finger at other people's failures as a convenient cloak for our own. God is fixed in good, the devil in evil; but man is in between, on the road of evil but with an ear still open to the good.

But the devil did not create us; he stole us. Yet God knew what He was doing from the beginning. He foreknew what would happen, we are told, and had made His preparations. He knew that man was going to fall before He created him (1 Pet. 1: 20). We may therefore be equally sure that He who foreknew all things knew that those heavenly beings who lost their first estate and first opened the kingdom of darkness, would do this very thing. And what God foresees, He foreplans (Acts 2:23 and Eph. 1: 11).

There is a point here which is probably not reconcilable to the human mind—the fine line between "the determinate counsel and foreknowledge of God" and any implication that God was responsible for the origin of evil. We need not stop to deny anything so obvious as the latter, but we can gain much benefit by grasping the certainty of the former. God foreknew the coming of evil into the universe both by the fall of angels and of man; it all had its place in the plan of Him "who worketh *all* things after the counsel of His own will", and He had already made full provision for an outcome a million times more glorious than if there had never been a Satan and sin. Indeed, the Scripture plainly states that He deliberately subjected His creation to its bondage of corruption, to its groaning and travailing, to "nature red in tooth and claw", in view of the overwhelming glory of the outcome (Rom. 8: 20, 21). Strong words. And this much we can see: there would be no means of demonstrating the true character of love which lays down its life for its enemies, which overcomes evil with good, which blesses those who curse it, if there were no enemies, no evil, no curses. And in our own lives we know, by Scripture and by experience, that it is our temptations which drive us into the cleft of our Rock; it is our sufferings which divorce us from the world and stabilize us in Christ: it is our frustrations and oppositions which give Him the opportunity to manifest His patience and love through us. If we were not harassed by temptation, we should not learn the lessons of abiding: if we were not faced with difficult situations, we should not practise the faith that overcomes them. So of this we are certain—that Satan never has had power or opportunity to take God by surprise, and to interfere in the smooth running of His creative plan and compel Him to change it. One day we shall find that Satan has been but an agent in God's unchanged, eternal purpose to crown His Son Lord of all and surround Him with the glorious inheritance of a redeemed humanity.

But if only One is to be glorified from eternity to eternity, only One must be the doer of all. If man has slipped into the quagmire of self-deceit, imagining himself to be somewhat by himself, deluding himself that he is a king, not a slave; then man must relearn that only One is King of kings and Lord of lords, and that at His name every knee must bow. He who, as Love, was Creator of all must now, as Love, be Re-Creator of lost mankind, and must bring him back by regeneration and re-education to the only relationship in which humanity can be true humanity.

4   RESTORATION IN ITS FIRST STAGE

LET us watch carefully how God has done this, so that ignorance of the ways of God may not rob us of our inheritance. First, it is God Himself who has done it, God, Father, Son and Holy Spirit, "God our Saviour", as Paul loved to call Him; God alone, that in all things He might have the pre-eminence. Not one grain of our re-creation in Christ is attributable to man, any more than our creation was. Man must learn, and re-learn, his eternal condition—the nothing over against the All. And what a relief! Not my past righteousness (non-existent), not my present works (wood, hay and stubble unless His works in me), not my future suitability (equally non-existent). All is His. His past planning, His completed redemption, His endless mercy and love.

First, God's righteousness must be satisfied. None but a righteous God could be God, nothing but righteousness could be the foundation of His throne. The broken law upon which His creation is based must have its penalties, if it is a law. If His eternal nature is to reward the good, He must also inevitably punish the evil. In no other way could He be righteous. No mere forgiveness, then, could be a just forgiveness, unless it was grounded on full satisfaction for the wrongdoing. What a Redeemer we have, who provided a salvation with no loopholes in it! Man's reasoning might and often does suggest some easier way, which is always, when traced to its roots, a subtle refusal to face the stark reality of lawlessness in a law-based universe. Abel knew it, when he first approached God with a blood sacrifice, the life of another symbolically shed for him. Cain, in the blindness of religious self-righteousness, offered his own good works, so much more pleasant and self-gratifying. But which touched reality? Which had the witness from God? The tragic end tells us, when Cain hated Abel for his glowing testimony to acceptance with God. And why did he hate him? John tells us (1 John 3: 12) because Abel struck at the roots of self-righteousness and exposed it as sin, which could only be expiated by God's appointed sacrifice, to which God bears faithful witness in the believer.

Here is salvation in its first stage, God's great salvation. The Judge became the condemned criminal. God the Son disguised His deity in human flesh, and "tasted death for every man". The Author and Sustainer of life yielded up His own life to receive in Himself the wages of the world's sin. As Mrs. Cousins put it in her great hymn:

> Jehovah lifted up His rod
>   O Christ, it fell on Thee!
> Thou wast sore stricken of Thy God;
>   There's not one stroke for me.
> Thy tears, Thy blood, beneath it flowed;
>   Thy bruising healeth me.
>
> Jehovah bade His sword awake,
>   O Christ, it woke 'gainst Thee!
> Thy blood the flaming blade must slake;
>   Thy heart its sheath must be—
> All for my sake, my peace to make;
>   Now sleeps that sword for me.

Through all eternity we shall never know what those hours meant when God was separated from God, the Son crying out to the Father, "My God, My God, why hast Thou forsaken Me?" But its glorious consequences we do know—that, having been "delivered for our offences", He "was raised again for our justification". The resurrection was God's witness that He had accepted the sacrifice. This was more than forgiveness. This was as if we had never sinned. God could now be just in justifying the believer in Jesus. We can leave the court without a stain on our character. Upon Another's life, Another's death, we can stake our whole eternity. The penalty of an eternal hell, the guilt, the stain, the rebellion, the broken law, the separation, all as if they had never been, for "Jesus paid it all".

This primary and fundamental aspect of the atonement is always represented in Scripture by the word "blood". "The precious blood of Christ." It is the first and necessary Godward side of the process of redemption. It was the solution, first, as we have said, of God's problem. How could He be just and the justifier of the unjust? *His* wrath must first be propitiated: *His* holiness vindicated: the punishment of *His* broken law inflicted. Nothing in the Bible stands out more prominently than the sacrifice God appointed and declared to be the satisfaction of all those claims. It was His own outpoured life. God as Spirit cannot be seen of men. God the Word and the Son, as the express image of the Father, could take human form, so "the Father sent the Son to be the Saviour of the world". We may know for certain that it cost the Father all and more than the Son to send Him to be the propitiation for our sins. The sacrifice was settled in heaven before the sin that necessitated it had appeared in history. The shedding of blood, representing the outpoured life of the victim, as

Moses declared in Leviticus 17, runs like a reddened strand throughout all Bible history—from Abel to Israel, where the life of the nation centred around the sprinkling of the blood on the annual day of atonement: on through the prophets to the last of them, the Baptist, who pointed to the Lamb of destiny and called Him God's Lamb "that taketh away the sin of the world": on through the great moment of the sacrifice itself hidden from all eyes in the three hours of darkness, proclaimed by the Saviour Himself to be His blood of the new covenant to be remembered at His table: expounded in fulness of revelation and understanding by the apostles: seen as presented and accepted by God Himself in the heavens in the letter to the Hebrews, giving us our title to boldness of access to the holiest of all: and consummated in the final vision of eternity, with the throne occupied by "the Lamb as it had been slain".

No wonder the blood is holy and precious to all believers. No wonder it is the point of attack and derision by those who hate to own themselves as sinners. It represents the uniqueness of that holy sacrifice, the blood He shed alone, the winepress He trod alone. It is His atoning work which none other shares. The cross, the manward aspect of Calvary's redeeming work, we share: the blood, the Godward aspect, is the sacred offering of the Son to the Father. And because He accepts it, we can do so. We need not question that sacrifice, nor its efficacy. He appointed it. He accepted it. He invites, He argues, He commands us to do the same. No sinner pleases the heart of God by remaining a penitent. No, if repentance is sincere, let us not add sin to sin by failing to believe in the blood. If good enough for Him, it is good enough for us. Nothing pleases the Father more than the faith of a sinner in the efficacy of the precious blood.

5   MAN'S BASIC FACULTY

THIS groundwork of our salvation is received only by revelation. "Hereby know we the Spirit of God: Every spirit that confesseth that Jesus Christ is come in the flesh is of God." This, wrote John, is the revelation of revelations. Who could conceive of it, who could believe it? The proud human heart never can and never will, for it leaves man with no shred of self-justification. God alone could do for us what we could never do for ourselves, and God took flesh to do it. No one really believes this, although we may say we do, until the Spirit of God reveals it to us; and the Spirit can only reveal it, when He has first given us a glimpse of what we really are in the sight of God; and that also is by revelation. Means He uses—the Bible, preaching, personal witness, the lives of living Christians, sometimes disappointments, loss or sorrow; but the light has to shine, and we respond to it; and that very response is a conviction of the Spirit which we cannot escape. We at last realize what we are and admit it. That is what the Bible calls the gift of repentance, the change of mind concerning ourselves, such a change affecting conduct and producing what the Bible calls "works meet for repentance".

This gift of repentance is really the reverse side of that one fundamental response God quickens in us—faith. It is the quickening or re-directing of the one automatic faculty with which the creation is endowed, as well as being the most elementary and utterly simple—the faculty of reception. We have sought to make it clear from the beginning that the Creator-creature relationship is in the nature of things of one kind only, that of giving and receiving. The Creator gives all by giving Himself, the creature receives all; and the faculty of receiving is so simple, obvious, natural, automatic, that it can hardly be called an action at all. It is the first activity of a newborn babe, receiving air, receiving nourishment. It is the continued activity which sustains all life. And that is faith. The repentance side of faith is in essence the breaking down and giving up of a false faith which we have received from Adam, a faith in our own self-righteousness, our own religion, our own philosophy; the receiving of a false self-reliance as a basis of living; thus it is the negative side of faith, the saying no to an illusory faith.

Positive faith, which Paul speaks of as "the gift of God" (Eph. 2: 8), is now the further glorious revelation by the Spirit of the shed blood of Christ as the propitiation for the sins of the world, attested to by the Scriptures, and the consequent simple reception of Jesus as crucified and living Saviour, and our acceptance with God through Him. The receptive faculty which has spued out what it used to drink in, its own righteousness, now with simple delight receives in its place and drinks in the living waters of salvation through Christ. What is called faith can hardly be called a work, because it is so automatic that we humans hardly realize we are exercising it. In the normal activities of life we do not think of ourselves as exercising faith when we receive something; we are more occupied with the object we are receiving; and if we want it, we just take it; the act of taking is so simple and obvious it hardly counts in our consciousness. Whether it be air or food or sitting on a chair or receiving a present, if we want a thing and it is available to us, the taking of it is automatic: and that is faith. So also in the realities of the Spirit. They are gifts indeed, because they are beyond the reach of fallen reason, beyond the sight of blinded eyes. They are direct revelations from another world, mediated to us through the Word made flesh and the Word written; but as they penetrate our consciousness by the power of the Spirit, negative and positive faith go into automatic action, rejecting the former false assumptions, and accepting their glorious replacement—the righteousness of Christ by faith, acceptance in the Beloved, adoption into the family of God. We are "born from above".

In thus seeking to outline the primary operations of the Spirit, and man's response, I have deliberately aimed at keeping clearly before us the fundamental fact that God acts for ever according to His eternal nature, and man according to his, and that this must be invariable in both. God for ever gives, man for ever receives. In the glory of His grace, that is what God never ceased to do: "He giveth, and giveth, and giveth again." Therefore salvation, just as much as creation, is every iota a gift. And man, of whom it is said concerning his creation, What hast thou that thou hast not received?, can never experience the abc of his re-creation in Christ until he is brought back to the act of simple reception. As Jesus said, "Except ye become converted and become as little children, ye cannot enter the kingdom of heaven." Every iota of works, of self-effort, has to disappear. Faith, so far from being works, is really only the flash of recognition of what is: in this case, already redeemed, if we only knew it. I hope I have made this clear, because it is the first infant experience of the lost secret of humanity, a secret we shall never outgrow and never replace, for it is humanity's sole basic capacity.

6

WHAT REALLY HAPPENS AT REGENERATION?

AND now, what really happens at the new birth? It is most important to understand. Remember again that the creature has no other end to his existence than to be a manifestor of the Creator—God in man, and God through man; and that therefore a human being is not a true human until he is a temple of the Holy Spirit. Nothing can function except by the laws of its being; a car won't go unless its machinery works aright; and a man can never be a man unless he is a God-indwelt, God-controlled man, because men are not made to "work" any other way. That is why life is a jigsaw puzzle until the Masterhand pieces it together; that is why "there is no peace, saith my God, to the wicked", because the wicked are all of us who still have a dethroned God and an enthroned self at our centre, and "the wicked are like the troubled sea, when it cannot rest". Nor can there be any possible purpose in a redemption for man, unless it is to restore his humanity to the only condition in which it slips into gear. Remember God CANNOT create a creature except, in its measure, to contain and shew Him forth: "God is seen God in the star, in the stone, in the flesh, in the soul and the clod." Of the lower forms of creation, animate and inanimate, who are without choice in the matter, it is written, "The whole earth is full of His glory." Man, however, in the height of his privilege, made in the similitude of God, with faculties like His though not with the incommunicable attributes of His Godhead, has had the awful responsibility of intelligent choice. Created free to choose his glorious destiny of being the conscious container and transmitter of God, he could and did refuse, and thus became the child of the devil, the original rebel. There can, then, be only one possible purpose in God's grace in salvation—to restore man to his sole and original destiny—"Christ in you, the hope of glory."

We stress this again because the only infallible, inexorable consequence of a sinner receiving salvation is not always made plain by Gospel preachers. It is often easy to get the impression that it is certainly necessary to have our sins forgiven, to be delivered from the wrath to come, to receive an assured entrance into heaven; but to submit to the total control of Christ is something which may and should follow, but does not necessarily do so; and even that it is possible to enjoy the former without the latter. Nothing could be more false or absurd. There is no salvation conceivable, possible or actual, other than God's way in infinite grace of destroying the false form of life in which man lives, and replacing it by the true. The false form of life is that which has self in the centre, which is the sin in which my mother conceived me, which is the false god. The true form of life is that which has God at its centre—Christ living in me.

It is for that reason Paul used the striking expression in Gal. 1: 17 to describe his conversion—"when it pleased God . . . to reveal His Son *in* me". The startling fact is that on the road to Damascus it was the exalted Christ who spoke to him from heaven; yet he writes years afterwards that the outcome of God's dealings with him those three eventful days was not an external revelation of an ascended Christ, but an internal revelation of the Indwelling Son. The eternal life which had begun in Paul was not some "thing" received in a detached sense as a gift from the heavenly Father; but the start of an eternal union. One more human soul, a deluded, blinded captive of the great egoist, Satan, impregnated from birth with his evil spirit of egoism, had now been led captive by Him who "leads captivity captive"; which meant that with Paul's deliverance from that Satanic spirit of egoism at the cross, another Ego, the Great I Am, Jesus the Son of God, had begun to live His life within the little, emptied ego of Paul.

In other words, and let us get this clear, the atoning work of Christ, which makes it possible for a lost sinner to stand in the sight of God as one who had never sinned, is only the gateway to life, not the life itself. The life itself is, and can never be anything but, Jesus Himself, "that eternal life which was with the Father and was manifested unto us", coming into the cleansed vessel, occupying His holy temple, being the life of the branch now attached to the Vine, the life of the member of the body now attached to the Head.

Do we see the point? Salvation is only salvation when it is God—Father, Son and Holy Spirit—returning to live in the personality created for Him, but exiled from Him through the fall. This is the inner reality of such parables as the prodigal returning to his Father. Therefore salvation is only salvation to any individual believer when the Spirit has given the inner witness of the presence of the Indwelling Christ. It is certainly true that a new born babe in Christ might not be able to interpret his new living experience in these exact terms; but it *must* be true that he has not merely an external faith in a Christ crucified 2000 years ago, but also, as the inevitable result of the heavenly gift of repentance toward God and faith toward our Lord Jesus Christ, the inner revelation of "Christ in me", *my* Saviour, *my* Lord, evidenced by an inner witness that is both incomprehensible to the world, and indescribable. That is the sole and only purpose of the atonement, and the inevitable effect of true repentance and faith, which neither man nor devil can prevent.

7 THE ROOT IS DEALT WITH

BUT in actual fact something much more radical has taken place than a convert is often either taught or realizes; and the failure to realize the true meaning of God's dealings with us results in a weak birth or stunted growth. Our real problem has never been the sins we have committed, but the sinner who commits them. It is this infected ego, this deified self in me, of which my sins are only an outward expression. If I lose my temper, if I hate or resent, if I lie or respond to a lust, it is my infected "I" which has done it because it likes to—that is my basic trouble. It is this "I" which has been the hateful false god in the usurped temple of my personality. It is this "I" which all men really worship, unless it has been exchanged for the great I AM. It can be a most respectable "I", for a certain amount of respectability is a pleasant clothing for it and only seats it all the more firmly on its false throne. Love for one's own family, class, or nation, morality, religion can all be its clothes. It has its unpleasant side, for it is a slave to its own lusts, passions and ambitions, and shoulders other selves out of its way to obtain them; but on the whole it can progress fairly well, if it can preserve the eleventh commandment, "Thou shalt not be found out"!

Now this is the nerve-centre of the trouble which must

be eliminated. It must be destroyed; nothing short of that will do. It is not the original self which must be destroyed. That would be absurd; God made that to be His dwelling-place, His co-operator, His fellow. It is the spirit of *independence in the self*, the virus in the self, producing a self that lives unto itself and by itself, the self that has turned in on itself. In other words, it is not the self which must be destroyed, but the Satanic spirit of egoism in the self. It is like an iron cage in which all humanity is confined; it is like iron shackles which none can break. All the religions of the world try to break it; but the prisoner cannot release himself. All they can exhort man to do is to free himself by his own efforts, good resolutions, religious observances, good works, service to others. But helpless human self is always a slave (Rom. 6: 16), and can never deliver itself: it was not created capable of doing so.

Only the living God has given the remedy, and it comes from outside, down from above. It could neither be known, nor conceived of, nor experienced, except from without, for from within it would be still fallen self. But God Himself, the primal Self, who was from eternity the selfless Self, the wholly Other from the fallen self, the outgoing Self, He who is love, took flesh and became man. He entered into the closed circle of this perverted world, a real man born of woman, measuring up to the plumbline of His own perfect law from which He never deviated a fraction, overcoming not by that will-o'-the-wisp of man's vain imaginations—self-effort—but by knowing His human nothingness and the allness of His indwelling Father (John 14: 10). He was then in a condition to be what none but the Sovereign Creator could be—the end of the old and the beginning of the new. Coming as God's representative man, to whose coming that former representative man, the first Adam, had pointed in his failure (Rom. 5: 14), coming as God's last Adam to end the old race and found the new and final one, He did the only thing that the New Founder could do, the thing which had been fore-shadowed through the blood sacrifices and burnt offerings of history. As representative of all humanity, just as much as an ambassador represents his whole nation in what he says and does, He died a representative death, and rose to a representative new life. The Scripture says He was "made sin for us" (2 Cor. 5: 21), and that touches bottom. In other places it says He bore our *sins*, but here, He was "made *sin*", made the very thing in itself. But what is sin? Self-centred egoism, of course. Sin appeared when Lucifer said "I will" in defiance of the "I will" of God; when he chose to be his own self-sufficient god in place of contain-ing the living God. That independent "I" was sin. Sin in essence is not a thing, not a taint, but a person, the evil spirit of independent selfhood, just as holiness is not a thing, but *The* Person, the Holy Spirit. And when Jesus was "made sin", the thing-in-itself, He, representing us all, became egotistic humanity, infected with that satanic spirit. All that abominable, rebellious, hateful indepen-dent self clothed Him there, and He was *made* it. Why? Because the human self must *die* to the false, if the true is to replace it. And it died to it in Jesus, died utterly, died absolutely. When that holy body was buried as a corpse, and that same body was "raised again", "this same Jesus" had died to *sin* (Rom. 6: 10), as well as died *for* sins; the same Person, representing us all, had become once and for all separated in death from that evil spirit of independent self, and had risen possessed by another Spirit, the Holy Spirit of God.

It is no mere figure of speech, no theological theory when the Scripture says, "We thus judge that if one died for all, then were all dead." Spiritual realities are the true realities, and unchanging: and there is no greater reality in history than the death of Christ on the cross, and its effects. We say again, this is not something we read in a book, but real fact; not something real in Christ "positionally" in the heavenlies, but real actually on earth. When Paul said, "Then were all dead", and "Ye are dead", and "We that are dead to sin", and "Your old man is crucified with Him", he meant exactly what he said.

What then died, when Christ as sin, as representative egoist, died? Death is never a dissolution, disappearance: it is a separation, a transference from one dimension of living to another, from one environment to another. So self did not die, for God made self to function in perfection in its right relationship to Him, the Creator Self. It was the separation of the human, created self from the false spirit of egoism and self-sufficiency of the self that took place in Christ's death to sin for us; separation from that thing of which devils are made and which is the sole characteristic of hell. That iron band was broken, the prison house destroyed in the *power* of that mighty death. When He died, He died to that in our place. There could be no other effective remedy; death to the false must take place, separation from it, and it did—in Christ.

But then what lives when Christ arose? Self in its original, primal relationship to God. This is seen in the resurrection of Christ, in that He did not, could not as representative man, rise by Himself; for human selves are not created capable of doing things by themselves, and He died and rose as a man for our sakes. So He "was raised up from the dead by the glory of the Father", by "the Spirit of Him that raised up Jesus from the dead" He was "put to death in the flesh, but quickened by the Spirit". And the new man in Christ is the helpless self quickened and indwelt by the Spirit. The implication of this we will see later.

But back first to our Representative in His death. "If one died for all, then were all dead." Can we actually accept that as a personal fact? Is it a fact in me? It is not only a fact in me, but in every one who has saving faith in Christ. A book by L. E. Maxwell has the title, *Born Crucified*. That is true, for everyone who is born of God is born in no other way than by Christ being born in him, Christ becoming his new life, Christ becoming the new Self in his redeemed self. But that is only possible and actual because the Christ to whom we have become spiritually united is the Christ who first died as our representative and took into death the world's falsely infected ego, which included my falsely infected ego. Therefore the first effect of our union through faith is the separation in His death of my ego from its false infection. This is the meaning of the greatest passage of Scripture on this subject, Rom. 6: 1–11. The proof that this is a fact, is that no born-again man is the self-centred man he once was. He is "a new creation", and he knows it. The very fact that he knows it is proof of his new birth, for those who are still fast bound in their fallen selfhood cannot know it; they are blind to any other dimension of life: "the natural man receiveth not the things of the Spirit of God; for they are foolishness unto him; neither can he know them, for they are spiritually discerned". But when in Christ those iron bands were broken and we are born anew, we can look back and plainly discern between what we were in our unsaved condition, and what we are now, for "he that is spiritual judgeth all things". Let us make no mistake. We have *died*, so far as being the egocentric pervert we were from our mother's womb, we have risen, the same person yet an altogether new man in Christ. Something that once was is no more. "Our old man is crucified with Him", "ye are dead with Christ", "we are buried with Him"—all statements in Rom. 6.

What then are we to do about it? Do what humans can only do—receive facts, rejoice in them, act as possessing them. We say again: Every born again believer is a crucified believer. They may not have realized it, because "the whole counsel of God" in its full range of revelation is so often not taught to believers. But whether they realize its implications or not, whether they understand their true position in Christ or not, they are living a new life which is Christ-centred and not self-centred, or they are not born again; and they can look back and plainly distinguish between what they were and what they are: and that is actual death and resurrection.

8   WHAT REALLY IS THE NEW MAN?

BUT now let us pass on to the resurrection side, and then later go back and seek to tie the two together. There is indeed a subtle lesson to learn here, and failure to recognize it, and the consequent confusion is, I believe, the greatest cause of the entanglements in both our Christian living and knowledge.

We have already stressed that the Scripture makes it plain that the last Adam, the Progenitor of the new race, the Saviour who ended the old by taking it into His death, and began the new by His resurrection, did not rise by His own efforts or power. For our sakes He had become the first Man of the new nation, "the firstborn among many brethren"; and men cannot do things by their own efforts. Therefore when we speak of the new man, we mean a people who have an entirely and radically new conception both of the powers and function of the human personality, a people "renewed in the spirit of their minds". Whereas they previously thought in terms of self-sufficiency and self-effort, now they use the same language about themselves as the Saviour on earth about Himself, when He said, "The Son can do nothing of Himself", and Paul when he wrote of himself "who am nothing", and the disciples to whom Jesus said, "Apart from Me, ye can do nothing." They have had a divine revelation of the created helplessness and nothingness of the human self. But that alone is not enough. Even as, through faith, we have been joined to a dead and buried Christ, so far as our old selves are concerned; so have we also been joined to a risen Christ so far as our new selves are concerned, and so joined to Him that we are one: "he that is joined to the Lord is one spirit". And that means nothing less than the new man being Christ and I made one, and in that union He is the all, and I the nothing; He is the Vine, the living tree, I the branch, the appendage to the tree, which it vitalizes with its sap, and through which it produces its fruits. Therefore for all essential purposes the new man is Christ: "Christ who is our life", "Christ is all and in all".

The perfect Scriptural presentation of this relationship, given in complete and masterly outline with almost the stroke of a pen, and yet weaving together all the intricate threads that make the pattern of the new life in Christ, is Gal. 2: 20: Paul's master analysis of his own condition as a new man in Christ. The first half of that verse will repay unceasing study, until the Spirit illuminates in personal understanding and experience the fundamental and subtle balance of truth in the three operative statements—"I am crucified with Christ": "nevertheless I live": "yet not I, but Christ liveth in me".

The first is clear, in the light of what we have already been seeing of the death of Christ and of ourselves in Him. The "I" which has been crucified with Christ is, of course, the old egocentric self with which we came into the world.

The second—"nevertheless I live"—is the new Paul, our new selves, risen from the dead in Christ, the same self as before so far as our organs and faculties are concerned, but "renewed in the spirit of our minds", "created in righteousness and true holiness", the dead and risen self to which Paul refers when he says, "Reckon ye *yourselves*

to be dead indeed unto sin, but alive unto God . . .
yield *yourselves* unto God as alive from the dead." This
renewed "I" has a pure heart (Acts 15: 8; 1 Pet. 1: 22), a
purified soul (1 Pet. 1: 22), pure mind (2 Pet. 3: 1),
dedicated body (Rom. 6: 13; 12: 1) the temple of the Holy
Ghost.

But then Paul definitely qualifies this second statement
by a third: "Yet not I, but Christ liveth in me." Why does
he do this? Because the real new I is Christ in me. That is
the crux of the matter, and takes us right back to where we
started. We saw that God Himself, He alone, is the All—
the eternal life, light, love, wisdom, power, holiness. And
He *can* only make creatures to contain Him. He cannot
make other gods who are self-existent with all the attributes of the godhead, for then He would cease to be God
alone. He *can* only create receivers, containers, and
manifestors of Himself. And this is equally true of man,
the summit of His creation, intelligent creatures with
faculties like Himself with whom He can have fellowship
and who can be His sons. They too can only be recipients
and containers and manifestors of the One God. That
alone is their highest privilege and the limit of their
capacity. Therefore when the God of all grace redeems
man from his false, deceived, imagined, impossible so-
called life of self-centredness, He can only redeem him by
ridding him of this false attitude and restoring him to the
true and only function of his humanity, to be the recipient
and container of the Living God. And this, in the glory of
His grace, takes place in our faith-union with Christ in
His death and resurrection. Through the mighty power of
His cross the "old man", Satan-infected, dies; through the
mighty power of His resurrection the new man, which is
Christ in us, Christ the all, we the nothing, lives.

But, in the perfect balance of Paul's statement, the dual

consciousness in the new man must be carefully noted. It does not just say, "Christ lives in me"; but "I live" *and* "Christ lives in me". And it continues about "the life I now live in the flesh", but that it is lived "by the faith of the Son of God". There is a distinct division of consciousness between "I" as the new man, and "Christ in me". Jesus, as a Man, had that same consciousness in the Garden, when He prayed, "Not as I will, but as Thou wilt." Now in the final resurrection of the body, when we shall be "like Him", when we shall all together have become one "perfect man", Head and body, when we shall be beyond the reach of temptation, as God Himself now is (James 1: 13), we will no longer have this divided consciousness, for it is a product of the fall which replaced the single knowledge of good with the dual knowledge of good and evil.

9   THE PROBLEM OF DUALITY—GOOD AND EVIL

W^E will diverge for a moment to look more closely into this problem of good and evil; but the contents of this chapter may possibly divert the attention of the reader from the main channel of the message of this book, and may be of interest to only a few. Readers, therefore, will lose nothing if they pass straight on to the next chapter.

The tree of the knowledge of good and evil, the taking of whose fruit destroyed for humanity the single consciousness of good and replaced it with the divided consciousness of these two opposing forces, opens a window, I believe, into the very structure of life as we know it: how it was made to function, how it has gone wrong, and how it must be restored.

Life, as known to us, is universally duoform; we can conceive of no other basis to all knowledge, sensibility, and activity. Every known thing has its reverse side, and is only known by contrast with its reverse. We see it in positive and negative, light and dark, male and female, bitter and sweet, and so ad infinitum, right up to God and man. These pairs of opposites are not enemies, but friends; each pair is one unit, the one in each pair being the mate of the other. Each is necessary to the other, just as much as each is indissolubly part of the other. Their interplay, their union, the one with the other, but *in the right pro-*

portion of each, is the source of all manifestation. Thus the mingling of sweet and not-sweet (bitter) in their varying proportions produces all the varieties of taste. The shining of light on solid substances which are not-light (darkness) produces all the beauties of form and colour. The friendly opposition of positive thinking in one direction to negative thinking in all other directions makes all the decisions of life; for if we say yes to one line of action, it is because we are at the same time saying no to all others. If we love one thing, it is because we hate any other things opposed to it. It is what philosophers have named the dialectical relationship, the thesis and its anti-thesis which form the synthesis. But what has to be noted is that in all the infinite number of pairs of opposites the positive is the dominant, and the negative the dominated element; the positive is the male nature, the negative the female.

In their love union the female's relationship to the male is that of submission. She is necessary to him, to receive his seed, and that his child may take form in her womb, but the child born is *his* child, and takes *his* name. Look again, for instance, at sweet and not-sweet (bitter). Sweet is the dominant, the positive, the male element; but all varieties of pleasant tastes are only in existence because the sweet is mingled with its opposite, its female, the negative, the not-sweet (bitter): the not-sweet gives proportion and reality to all these varieties. But the sweet is the dominant factor, the male, and all these varieties are its children. In yes and no, when a decision must be made, yes must be the dominant; but to make the positive decision, there has been a union with the no to all other possibilities; the all-embracing negative has been the mother which has given form and birth to the one positive.

In all these pairs, each opposite being part of its one

whole, there is no disharmony; they are as husband and wife to each other, their interaction, each in its right proportion, reproduces their children of form and taste and colour, of deed and word, in fact of all manifest life. Polarization, the interaction of the positive and negative electrical forces in the atom, is the same principle in the basic structure of the universe. God and man are, by the grace of His creation, in the same relationship. Without His opposite, His creature, the female to His male, the wife to the Husband, the body to the Head, He cannot manifest Himself. He is the positive. We are the negative, the not-God. Joined to Him in rightful submission, we die to ourselves, we say no to ourselves, and in doing that, His seed, which is Christ, is sown in us, formed in us and reproduced by us. Here the union is complete. It is symbolized for us in Scripture in the Head and body, Bridegroom and bride relationship of Christ and His church.

But the trouble has been in that one form of the negative creation in which there could be a potential disunity with its positive, for it has intelligence and free will— angels and men. Here something has happened which has vitiated and disordered all the properties of life, and turned harmony into disharmony. The negative has opposed itself to the Positive, rivalled it and rebelled against it.

Indeed these "negative" created beings have acted as if they could exchange places with their Positive, and the creature act as the Creator, the female as the male. That has meant that the activities of the rebel negatives have had to be given positive names. What should be just a negative not-good has become positive evil. Not-light has become a positive power of darkness; the creature, who is the not-God, has been perverted and become a positive devil. That is why we come to regard evil, darkness, hate, lust and so on as positively bad things, and they are called so in the Bible. They *are* bad and eternally bad, and produce their eternally bad fruits, and have their eternally bad sphere of existence in God's outer darkness and lake of fire. But in their original form they were merely the negatives of their respective positives and positive evil was meant to be non-existent.

The created beings, angels or men, should have been saying: "We are the not-good, not-God, not-light, not-wise. We know our emptiness (not-fulness). Knowing that we are the negatives, we delight to be filled with the one who is the Positive, the Good, the Wisdom, the Light, and that in and through our not-fulness He will manifest His fulness. We will be female to His male, receive and reproduce His allness, His beloved Son, through our nothingness." The obedient negative, in other words, instead of remaining a submissive emptiness to be filled with the Positive, the living God, was changed into a harmful, virulent, active so-called positive rebel.

That has necessitated God's declared and manifested "no" to all that is the active opponent to Himself. His "yes" to all love, goodness, and light—the characteristics of His own self-giving self—has necessitated His "no" to this rival kingdom of evil, to His created beings who, instead of accepting their created condition of not-fulness to be filled by Himself, have changed themselves into self-loving selves, with the negative characteristics of not-good, not-love, not-light, becoming positive evil, lust and darkness. This "no" of God is His necessary hate of and judgment on all these perversions, the not-true, not-real (in its final essence), not-righteous, and His hell for those who persist in their blind delusion that the false is a form of truth and the darkness a form of light, and the non-real a form of reality. To such, hell will be real indeed through all eternity where they dwell in the dark fire of their rebellious negative natures.

In this way division and opposition has arisen between the Creator and His created beings, and it has spread through and infected all the creation. That is the tree of the knowledge of good *and evil*. We live in a divided world.

10 SELF-CONSCIOUSNESS AND CHRIST-CONSCIOUSNESS

W E are desperately conscious of the two opposing principles of good and evil through all life. They confront us in human nature, in the business, political and social world. They give rise to the constant tensions among nations, races, classes, right down to our own family circles. They are the theme of ethics and religion. They come closest home to us in our own personal lives, the conflict of flesh and spirit, the interweaving of prosperity and adversity, joy and sorrow, friendship and enmity, justice and injustice, health and disease, kindness and cruelty, through the whole garment of life. Now, though we are Christ's, we share in this divided world. We are part of it. We eat its food, partake in its activities, earn its money, taste of its sorrows and tragedies, endure its temptations. Though one'd with Christ in spirit, we are still one with the world in body. Therefore, though new men in Christ, we still have a duality of consciousness: we have self-consciousness, world-consciousness, flesh-consciousness as well as Christ living in us. Not that it is wrong to be self- or world-conscious, we are in the world (but not of it: John 17: 13, 16), in the flesh (but not of it: Gal. 5: 24), in self (but not of it: Gal. 2: 20). A great proportion of our waking hours must necessarily be spent in the affairs of this world, with Christ in the background rather than foreground of our consciousness. Sin only enters when we are consciously drawn into

activities and attitudes which we know to be displeasing
to Him. While we are in this divided world, we cannot
have solely a Christ-consciousness. We must also have a
self-consciousness; certainly it is the renewed self which
knows how to maintain its abiding place; yet it is also a
self-conscious self, responsive to all the stimuli of its
environment, therefore as open to temptation fleshward
as to Christ-control spiritward. It is still a case of "nevertheless I live", as well as, "yet not I, but Christ liveth
in me".

The name God has given to humanity separated from
Himself by the Fall—is "flesh" (Gen. 6: 3). We are all flesh.
Even the Saviour, when He came to be among us, was
"God manifest in the flesh". Not until the resurrection of
the body, the final and complete state of unification with
our ascended Head, can any member of the human race
cease to be flesh. Flesh implies consciousness of separation
from God, self-consciousness apart from Christ-consciousness. That does not necessarily mean something
evil. Christ "in the days of His flesh" was conscious of
His human self as apart from the Father with whom He
was one (e.g. John 5: 19). It is not flesh which is evil, but
the lusts of the flesh. And even they are not evil unless they
are permitted to reign instead of serve. Self-consciousness,
flesh-consciousness, is the normal and essential prerequisite, as members of this fallen human race, to a
continuous life of faith, for it compels us constantly to
"look away" from our helpless selves unto Jesus (Heb.
12: 2): and as we do so, flesh then becomes the servant
and manifestor of Spirit. But the moment we fail to look
away, then flesh becomes an evil thing, natural "desires
of flesh and mind" have us in their grip, and become
dominating, discordant lusts, and we their slaves.

Here, then, we come back to our former consideration

—the dual consciousness of Paul and all of us that, though made anew, with Christ as our life, we *are* conscious of two selves, ourself and Himself: "I live, yet not I, but Christ liveth in me"; because we are still members of a fallen, divided human community, the world of man. But the fact that we have human constitutions, human appetites and passions, human and corruptible bodies, and are immersed in all the human activities of this divided world, does not mean that we still have the fallen nature; it died with Christ; we have the *human* nature, and are not yet clothed with "the building of God, an house not made with hands, eternal in the heavens"; with a nature so completely unified that there will be no consciousness of separation, of good and evil, of temptation.

Our present privilege is to be God's redemptive agents, in every faculty and appetite responsive to our environment, for by us men God now offers His grace to men, even as by a Man He redeemed man; therefore, as humans among humans, we are as open as Jesus was through our human natures to all human enticements, as in our spirits to the drawings of the Spirit. As Paul tells us, we "walk in the flesh" (2 Cor. 10: 3), but so far as our real life in the Spirit is concerned, we "have crucified the flesh" (Gal. 5: 24), and are "not in the flesh, but in the Spirit" (Rom. 8: 9), and do "not war after the flesh" (2 Cor. 10: 3), and do not "mind the things of the flesh" (Rom. 8: 5). In other words, once again we are in the flesh, but not of it, in the world but not of it, and in self, but not of it.

Therefore, let us get it clear, we shall never in this life be free from a sense of self, as well as a realization of the indwelling Christ. We shall never, therefore, be free from temptation in a world that exists to tempt, nor be free from the daily necessity of vigilance and abiding. The chapter of triumphant living, Rom. 8, significantly enough is the very chapter which warns against the subtleties of the surrounding flesh, and expresses our groanings amidst our rejoicing, as we long for the final redemption of the body, and are saved, not only by faith, but by hope.

For this reason, then, it is of utmost importance that we understand the exact relationship between the renewed self and the other Glorious Self, Christ Himself who dwells within. It is the hardest lesson we have to learn, and cannot be learned except in the hard way. Nothing but frequent and strong doses of the false activities of self can teach us this lesson. It is peculiarly subtle because it is now not a case of a troublesome *bad* self, but an anxious, frustrated, condemned *good* self; not good in the positive sense of being able to do good things, but good in the negative sense of wanting to do good and no longer wanting to do evil; a purified self, but though pure, still empty: just as a cup may be clean, but what really matters is the fluid it contains.

Our problem is that we have become so accustomed in our old life to the self-activity of the self, that we carry it over to the new life, hardly noticing that we do so. As we repeatedly say, the new man is actually Christ in us, we are merely the hidden filaments through which His light shines out, the cup which holds the water; as nearly as possible we don't count. We are ourselves conscious of this as we look in the face of our Beloved. We realize and recognize HIM as our life. Seeing Him, we just don't see ourselves. In our inner consciousness He is the life of our lives. But at the same time, we are immersed, of necessity, in worldly activities which demand every form of self-activity, and constantly, equally of necessity, divert us from conscious Christ-reliance. Our problem is how to live, naturally and freely, normal lives which are yet at their roots Christ living in and through us, even when for many of our waking hours our direct attention is centred on mundane affairs; and how to recognize sensitively and quickly when the pressure or sudden impact of things is pulling us off-centre on to self-reliance. It is what the writer to the Hebrews called "the dividing asunder of soul and spirit".

11   THE MEANING OF THE LAW IN SCRIPTURE

THE learning of this vital lesson Paul profoundly and vividly dramatized for us in Rom. 7. It is here that he writes so much about the law for the believer. What then is law?

It is plain from so many references to the law in Paul's writings that it has a very important place in his teachings. Indeed we soon find that the law is an essential component of the gospel. No law, no gospel. The one cannot be understood except in relation to the other; and in the final analysis we find that the one is the other! It is a dialectical relationship between them: the law is at the opposite pole to the gospel, and they are the negative-positive poles of the same Living Axis, the God of all life: for in Him both the "you must" of the law and the "you can" of the gospel have met in Christ.

First of all, then, we must rid ourselves of the commonly held idea that by the law Paul meant just the law of Moses, ceremonial or moral, and nothing else. The proof of that is his own varied use of the word, even to the point of apparent confusion; though as a fact those very variations compel us to seek and find the correct definition of law which is common to all these uses. In the letter to the Romans alone he speaks of "the law of faith", "the law of God", "the law of sin", "the law that when I would do good, evil is present with me", "the law of the Spirit of life in Christ Jesus", "the law of sin and death"; and in one verse (7: 23) three different uses—"another law in my members", "the law of my mind", and "the law of sin in my members". Plenty of room for confusion!

But not so, when we allow these varied uses of the word to direct our thinking from some special theological interpretation to its generally accepted meaning in daily life. When we speak of a law, we merely mean the definition and declaration of some particular aspect of universal truth. Or, to put it simply, a law is how a thing works, and it will work no other way. If we try to make it work differently, we suffer—that is all. The law of gravity, put in amateur terms, tells us that if we release an object held in our hand, it falls to the ground. That's how that law works. Defy it, deny it, drop the cup from your hand, and it falls and is broken. A law of mathematics says that two and two makes four. Deny it and reckon them as making five, and what happens to our household accounts? So a law is a convenient human method of defining an eternal, unalterable truth.

There are also temporary man made laws for the convenience of society, agreed methods of social behaviour with penalties attached to their infringement, which we call laws, such as the right or left of the road for traffic. But they can be regarded as a secondary and relative use of the word, with which we are not at present concerned.

Fundamentally, then, God Himself is the law, for both morally and materially the universe only works and can work by the fixed laws of its existence, and these are the outward expressions of the being of God; for God Himself can only be God and act as God according to the unchangeable laws of His own nature, the most basic of which is the supreme law: that "royal law according to the Scripture, Thou shalt love . . ." This means that all

D

creation can only function in certain ways, and will not work in any other way—and this is law.

But while the inanimate creation works automatically according to its laws—the law of physics, chemistry, biology, and so forth—when God came to the point of creating persons like Himself, with the freedom and intelligence which are the bases of personality, it was absolutely necessary for Him to make plain to their understanding the law of their being: that freedom spells responsibility, they are one and the same thing; for choice is inherent in freedom, you cannot have the one without the other; the free must choose, otherwise they are not free. It was therefore equally necessary to make plain to them what to choose and what not to choose, the way God's universe works and the way it does not work; and that is the origin of the law of God for man.

We do not know what means God took to enlighten the first created beings in the heavens concerning the laws of their being. We are only told of that one, Lucifer, who, with his great company of followers called in Scripture "the angels who lost their first estate", deliberately disobeyed the first law of his being—that he was only created, and could only be created, to contain and manifest the One. All we know is that he and his followers chose the way of self-deification, and thus broke the first fundamental law of submission to God, and received the consequent effects in themselves, becoming changed from angels to devils. It is obvious, therefore, that it must have been deliberate and intelligent choice, based on the knowledge of God's immutable law. We can there safely postulate this as the first known presentation of law to a created intelligent being.

We come to recorded historical fact when we read of the first pronouncement of law to a created human being in the Garden of Eden. It consisted of an explanation to Adam and Eve of the fundamental law of human life, with a direct warning against the possible breaking of it. This law (Gen. 2: 16, 17) made plain to them that created beings can only function by receiving the gifts of their Creator. They are on the receiving end of life, as we have explained all through these pages. So it was said, "of every tree of the garden thou mayest freely eat". The record has already told us that the most important of those trees was "the tree of life in the midst of the garden". If the pair had conformed to this fundamental law and lived only by receiving God's gifts, they would, as we have also previously explained, have ultimately desired and found their need of, not just the gifts, but the Giver Himself offered to them in the symbol of the tree of life. This would have brought them into the realized spiritual union of Creator with created, which is true humanity.

But, as with Lucifer and his followers, it was necessary that as free intelligent beings they should also be confronted with the possibility of a contrary choice, and its dire consequences, represented to them by the tree of knowledge of good and evil. By the law of their created being, they could never be more than helpless recipients, either controlled by the Spirit of life, or enslaved by the spirit of independent egoism, of self-love, the spirit of Satan, bringing them into captivity to all the chaotic instincts and appetites of the soul and body. Here was law in its first human origin, the law that governs created beings, made to receive and contain the Creator, but capable of receiving the opposite.

If Adam and Eve had moved on from receiving God's gifts to the ultimate goal of the Giver Himself, the moral and spiritual law would then have ceased to exist in any form of outward imposition upon them; for they would have been inwardly united to God who is the Law, and He through and with them would have lived His life of love, which is the fulfilling of the law. The choice would have been made which would have united them to the law living within them, the Living God Himself, and they would have become automatically keepers and doers of the law.

But now, through their transgression of this fundamental law, and the consequent separation of fallen humanity from God, a situation arose in which there had to be a substitute for the Living Law lived in them by God Himself. We have already explained that the fall of our first parents had not proceeded as far as the fall of Lucifer, for he had become fixed eternally in the false law of egoism, "the law of sin and death", and its eternal consequences. Adam and Eve, on the other hand, had obeyed that false law of Lucifer and had given themselves over to the control of the satanic spirit of self-love, but not yet to the point of no return. They were not yet out of earshot. They had not yet committed that sin against the Holy Ghost which makes it impossible to repent. Their vain hope had been, if possible, to have the best of both worlds, and at least that meant that they were still within reach of the voice of both judgment and mercy. God, therefore, immediately met them in the garden after their act of disobedience by law in a new form, by His inspoken word of both righteousness and abundant grace. Man was left with "the light that lighteth every man", the conscience, the work of the law which is written in all men's hearts (Rom. 2: 5). Here, then, is the law making its appearance in the history of fallen mankind from the beginning, not now as God the Living Law, expressing Himself through us as our natural life; but the law has now become something external to our nature imposed upon unwilling humanity in the form of commandments, and demanded of them as the only way by which human life can be lived, personally or nationally. But how different is the impact upon us of such laws, and the obedience they demand of us which cuts right across the grain of our selfish nature, from those same laws and commandments when "written on the fleshy tables of the heart" by the One who Himself is that law, and lives it in us! Nothing is wrong with the law, please note, not even with it in its dead and codified external form; Paul makes that plain in Rom. 7: 12, 13. The only wrong is our own change of attitude, which has made us the enemies instead of friends of God and His law, for "the carnal mind is enmity against God; it is not subject to the law of God, neither indeed can be".

But our God of mercy has stayed with humanity through the centuries. The law written on the hearts of all men became so stifled by sin even in those early times that it was practically choked out of existence, for "God saw the wickedness of man was great in the earth, and that every imagination of the thoughts of his heart was only evil continually" (Gen. 6: 5, 6). So He took further drastic steps of preservation leading to salvation for the human race, first in cleansing judgment through Noah and the flood, and then in preserving grace through Abraham and a chosen nation.

Israel now became the repository of His eternal law of righteousness (in other words, the only right way of life) and grace. What was written in men's hearts was now codified through Moses in the basic moral law of the decalogue, combined with a long series of laws of a more contemporary nature for the preservation of a right social and national life in the midst of the surrounding paganism: and all was imbedded in a wonderful series of ceremonial laws prefiguring the glory of His grace in the coming Redeemer, and making possible His holy presence among a sinful people through the types of the animal sacrifices.

But at this point the subtlety of the satanic spirit of egoism in man reached its height. Man could never fulfil the law, could never reach the unobtainable standard of "whosoever shall keep the whole law, and yet offend in one point, he is guilty of all", and avoid the condemnation of "cursed is every one that continueth not in all things which are written in the book of the law to do them". That was the whole point. It was to challenge him with the only principle of righteous living, and at the same time open his eyes to his own unrighteousness. "By the law is the knowledge of sin." "For God hath shut up all into disobedience, *that* He might have mercy on all" (Rom. 11: 32—Lit. trans.). It was what Paul called "the ministry of condemnation", "the ministration of death", which yet was "glorious", because it was the first stage in God's glorious work of redemption: for the gift of God's law was a gift of His grace, sent not to condemn but to save: for the law was to be "our schoolmaster to bring us to Christ". But so far from this massive presentation of the law of God being the means of condemnation to a law-breaking people, coupled with the means of grace through the sacrifices, for the most part the subtle egoism in man turned these into an exclusive religion of self-righteousness.

The law plunges its knife of conviction and condemnation right into the heart of our self-righteous selves, and produces one or other of two effects. Most, both in Israel and throughout the history of the church, hastily pluck out the knife and seek to heal the wound by the medicaments of self-justification, even to the point of using the worship and sacraments of the church as a covering of good works, anything indeed which will save them from the self-immolation of a broken and contrite heart, and will preserve their precious selves. These are they who by human philosophy, by social service, by religion, or alternatively by open antagonism or rationalism, "hate the light" and "will not come unto the light", and remain, though unacknowledged by themselves, under the condemnation of John 3: 19, 20. Some, on the other hand, "come to the light"; the knife does its killing work, and leaves their self-righteousness a corpse. From "going about to establish their own righteousness", they join the publican in his heart cry, "God, have mercy upon me, a sinner." In these the law has done its work and prepared the ground for faith in Christ.

So by the means of law, independent self has been exposed in its guilt and lawlessness. Here was Paul's first great teaching on law. It is God's elementary education (Gal. 4: 3; Col. 2: 20) "that every mouth may be stopped, and all the world may become guilty before God".

CHRIST then came to be "the end of the law for righteousness to every one that believeth". How did He do this, and what does it mean? First, let us carefully note that in His own human life, though "made of a woman, made under the law", He never for one moment up to Calvary was under the law in the sense of living His life by trying to keep an outward law. That is obvious, for the whole point is that that is a human impossibility. Helpless self, even unfallen self, can keep and do nothing of the works of God by itself. "The Son can do nothing of Himself," said Jesus of Himself. No, Jesus, as a man for our sakes, lived wholly by another law or principle: by the Father that dwelt in Him and did the works (John 14: 10). The Father, the Living Law, fulfilled the perfect law of His perfect nature of truth and love in and through the Son: by that means, and that means only, Jesus, the Son of man, lived the perfect life and completely kept the law.

But Christ had come to save humanity from a death-life in which, in our helpless, separated selves, we knew our responsibility to live the right way through the law written on our hearts, or codified before our eyes, but cannot fulfil it. So as our representative, He first bore in His own body the curse of the law, being made a curse for us. He endured all the penalty of the broken law on our behalf, and thus freed all who receive Him from its claims.

But He did more than that. He erased the very existence of a codified external law for all believers. When He arose from the dead, He left behind Him on the cross the whole entangling body of law with its demands as well as penalties, "abolishing in His flesh the law of commandments contained in ordinances", "blotting out the handwriting of ordinances that was against us, and took it out of the way, nailing it to His cross". For an external law is only in existence where there are those who do not fulfil the law by nature, but who can and may and do break it: "the law is for the lawless" (1 Tim. 1: 9). When people live the law by internal instinct, there is no outward law (Gal. 5: 23). External law only came into an existence when humanity began to live by its false god, the god of lawlessness, of independent self—"that wicked one". The moment, therefore, that humanity is restored to its predestined relationship of inner union with God, external law ceases to exist for it.

And this is what Christ did for us, making us "dead to the law by His body" (Rom. 7: 4). Being made sin for us, He died as sin-infected humanity; He arose as the new humanity who had died to sin, and this new humanity consists of all human beings who receive Him. He, then, who is the Living Law, becomes their life within, and lives the law within them. For them, therefore, the external law is buried. It is the old husband who has died in the crucified Christ, in Paul's bold symbolism of Rom. 7: 1–6, that we might be married to another, the risen Christ.

For the believer, then, the new creation in Christ, the holy nation, the whole idea of response to external law has faded into thin air. That kind of duty life, that elementary grade of living, only has to do with us when we are in the bondage of self-centredness and live the old life of self-effort, before we are born from above. In that condition, as we have seen, to preserve us from becoming fixed as devils, and to keep before our eyes the lode-star of godly living, for which we were destined, God gave us the dead formulas of a written law. Of course we could not keep them, nor wanted to, but confronted by them, if we were honest, we came face to face with our guilt (Rom. 3: 19). The law had completed our elementary education: our graduation was our admission of guilt. We now pass out of the school of the law for ever, into a new school—of faith. The fragments of law presented to us by Moses in His "ministry of condemnation" now become the completed Law, lived as a life by the Law-Maker, Law-Giver and Law-Keeper within us, the righteousness of the law is fulfilled *in* us, who walk not after the flesh but after the Spirit (Rom. 8: 4). The fruits of the Spirit, born by the Spirit through the believer as vine through branch, are the law lived, and "against such there is no law". Christ had lived the law on earth by the Living Law within Him, the Father dwelling within Him. Christ had removed all claims of broken law upon us by being made a curse for us on the cross: Christ now lives the law in us by His indwelling presence. Nothing of outward law has any further claim on the believer, for it was only the shadow of THE law, while we walked in shadow-land. Now the substance has come, The Law itself in us: when that which is perfect is come, that which is partial is done away.

But we still have a lesson to learn. The fact that we are dead to the external law by the body of Christ that we might be married to the Internal Law, Christ Himself, does not mean that external law has ceased to exist in the world. We live in the midst of it, surrounded by it, for we live in a world under judgment, under law, both for preservation and condemnation. It is very easy for us, therefore, to respond to the demands of the law, and by doing so, slip back almost unthinkingly to the false responses of self-effort. Added to this is the fact that all through our unregenerate days we have been so accustomed to self-effort as our only means of meeting the demands of this life, that we resort to it before we know where we are.

This is the reason why Paul returns to such a detailed discussion of the effects of law, this time on the believer, in Rom. 7. Some people have been puzzled by the appearance of Rom. 7 after Rom. 6, and thought it out of place. No indeed. For Rom. 7 is the law being used as a means of education for the believer, as it was for the unbeliever in Rom. 3. There it exposed his guilt, here his helplessness. There it pronounced judgment on the sins of the old man, here it exposes the subtle workings of sin in relation to the new man. Rom. 7 follows Rom. 6 just because it deals strictly and only with the problems of the new man in Christ, and has nothing whatever to say to the old man. This is fundamentally important for the understanding of the chapter. Rom. 6 is the old man out, cut off in Christ's death from the false spirit of egoism which dominated him, died in Christ to sin once for all. Just as the same Christ who had died as our representative rose, separated from that hateful infection with which He had been identified for our sakes, rose by the Spirit of the Father, rose the first new man of the new creation, the first-born from the dead; so we are new men in Him, separated from the old spirit of disobedience, indwelt by the Spirit of holiness. And from this crisis of faith in Rom. 6, by which we have recognized our new relationship of union with Christ and claimed it by faith, and connected ourselves to Him as risen from the dead, we now move on to the walk and warfare of faith in Rom. 7, 8, and on to the end of the letter.

But the start has to be this further stage in our education—the lesson of Rom. 7. We are not under the dominion of sin any longer only because we are not living by self-effort, but self-effort in the new man comes perilously easy to us just because we want to please God and delight now in His law, His standard of life. What more natural then, than to set about living by it? And at this point we have our new lesson to learn. We have discovered our guilt, now we must discover our helplessness. The new self is exactly as helpless as the old! It was created helpless, and never can be anything else! The only difference is that the old self, infected by the spirit of egoism, did not want to fulfil the laws of God, but the new self does (Rom. 7: 22). But neither can do it, nor are made to do it! And so the new self, all eager to please God, moves unwittingly into the trap and learns, as it has to learn, the hard way. Rom. 7: 7–13 tells us when Paul learned the lesson and how he learned it. Rom. 7: 14–24 opens to us the helpless bondage of the new self the moment it moves out of the vine-branch relationship, and endeavours to meet any claims on itself by itself. Not only can it not do so, but it finds another principle or law terrifyingly operative in itself. Self-effort *is* sin, it is self acting as its own god; therefore self-effort is immediately conscious of the domination of the selfish, lustful demands of its own appetites and instincts, and being helpless by nature cannot resist them.

This is why we said that Paul's answer to the problem of the oscillation between the self-conscious and Christ-conscious self, between soul and spirit, is an understanding of our relationship to law. It doesn't seem a relevant answer at first. But the point is that man's first and deepest instinct is not lawlessness, but law. That is to say, his first form of self-consciousness is *responsibility*. It was the first word spoken to him in the garden: "you must do this: you must not do that". It is the basis of personality. We are so used to thinking that sin is our primary problem. Paul goes deeper than that. He says that sin is a product of choice, and choice a product of responsibility, and responsibility is evoked by law. Man is a volitional creature: he must choose. What he chooses is secondary. Therefore man starts with law and his response to it.

Having made the first false choice which centred his life in self-effort, but having also an inescapable sense of responsibility as the very tap root of his nature, he still must face law—Thou shalt, Thou shalt not. He breaks the law, both because he wants to and because he cannot help it. But still law stands there confronting him. He is still a responsible being. If he turns to Christ and finds relief from the condemnation of the law, there law still stands with its unchanging demands. If now as a new man in Christ, ignorant of the true grounds of his new life, he still tries to obey the law, he is aghast to find that he still cannot obey it, and still is enchained by the contrary impulses of the flesh: till at last he echoes Paul's cry: "O wretched man that I am, who shall deliver me from the body of this death?" His basic problem, then, the problem of the new self, is not sin, but law. How can he escape these absolute standards confronting him? He cannot. How can he fulfil them? He cannot. So what? At last his eyes are opened. These are absolute standards. These are demanded eternally of him. But he has forgotten the first law "imposed" on him, the law (principle) of grace— that he should *receive* the grace of God, not that he should *do* anything of himself: and the grace of God is nothing less than the indwelling Law-Giver and Law-Keeper, keeping His own perfect law in the believer, the One who imposes the absolute standards on man being Himself the

One who maintains them in man: and that the only responsibility that man has is to receive Him, abide in Him, walk after Him. The puzzle is solved and every question answered. The external law, with its demands on self, has brought the believer to the end of his helpless self, until he has discovered that he has died to that law and had it replaced by the Internal Law, the indwelling Christ. Law, therefore, has completed its education, first of man's guilt, then of his helplessness: and only when the believer has learned this second lesson of how to refuse a false self-response to any demands of any outward law, and to replace it every time by abiding in the freedom of the guidance and control of the Law-Giver within, has he found the answer to the uprisings of self-reliance, self-reactions, self-effort in the daily life.

13 THE BELIEVER AND ROMANS 7

THIS, then, is the point of Rom. 7. We are out of the realm of the law and lawlessness in Christ's death and resurrection. That was the realm of God's elementary dealings with humanity. That was the realm of divided knowledge of good and evil, therefore of law and lawlessness. We have been lifted by grace into the realm of good alone, where Jesus is all; and all things, even evil things, work together for good. In this realm there is no divided heart, partly loving good and partly evil, part law and part lawlessness; but, like the men of old, all come with a perfect heart to make Jesus King, all love Him with heart and mind and soul and strength, and it is the Living Law fulfilling His righteousness in us.

But, let us say again, it is much easier said than done to keep ourselves out of the struggles and failures of Rom. 7, and in the liberties and victories of Rom. 8. Law and sin function only in the realm of independent self; for independent self is original sin. But we have become so accustomed to independent self-activities through our years in that realm, that it is as easy as can be to slip back into it; and that is, into Rom. 7. Instead of abiding in Christ and just quietly walking in Him, we take upon ourselves the pressures of duty, the demands of family, business, social or church service—and we have slipped back under law. We react to the minor irritabilities of life,

63

the fears, the things that go wrong, the people that upset us; we know we should not be stirred up by them; we endeavour not to be; but we fail, and are heavy-hearted with condemnation: we have slipped back under law. And under law means under sin, for the "strength of sin is the law", and the law is "weak through the flesh". In a combat between law and sin, sin wins every time; it has the mastery of us; for sin dwells in independent self, that is, in the flesh. This is always and immediately a fact in me, whenever I go back to my independent-self condition, forgetting my abiding place in Christ, and thus return, under the drive of the law. Sin, law's opposite, rises through my flesh, and I am temporarily a slave again, "carnal, sold under sin".

That is not my regular abiding place. No, indeed. We are "not in the flesh, but in the Spirit" (Rom. 8: 9). We are not under law, but have the Law-giver and Keeper fulfilling His own law of love in us. But, let us repeat: immersed, as we must be, in the affairs of a world under law, a world still in the elementary stage, we can so easily slip back into the domination of the law, through religious duties or service, through the affairs of home, society, business or nation, or through the common temptations of life; and when under law, we are in the flesh again, and back in Rom. 7, vainly struggling; for law only deals with men-in-themselves, seeking to function apart from Christ, and when we are that, even momentarily, there is the flesh, and there sin in the flesh.

Have we now got this clear? The old self crossed out in Christ. The new self redeemed in Him to be what it was created to be—a willing, loving, dependent manifestor of the Christ living within. But, not yet having attained the final goal of the union which will be ours, by grace, with the resurrection of the body, we are still mingled with a self-reliant world, and we are always liable in our new dependent selves to be diverted from Christ within to some form of self-reliance. In doing that, we enter again into the old conflict of the law with its demands on self, and sin-in-the-flesh with its opposition to the law; we are back in the struggling, striving and failing realm; for the new I, which delights in the law of God after the inward man, has to learn and re-learn its utter helplessness, according to the law of its creation, apart from Christ in it, and therefore its total defeat the moment it moves out of the shelter of "Christ in me". We have to learn, and learn deeply, that the new I, the "good" I, is as helpless as the old I, and is a slave to sin the moment it tries to manage its own affairs.

The law, then, fulfils two purposes. It reveals the presence of sin to the sinner, and pronounces his guilt (Rom. 3). It reveals the power of sin to the saint, and exposes his helplessness (Rom. 7). We can see, therefore, why, as the forerunner of Christ, it takes such an important place in Paul's exposition of the gospel, with a necessary ministration to sinner and saint, and yet one which must be done away with to make room for "the glory that excelleth". By it we receive a twofold ministry of condemnation, first as guilty sinners (Rom. 3: 19), with the guilt removed in the blood of Christ; then as failing saints (Rom. 7: 18) with the wretchedness removed by the new walk in the indwelling Spirit (Rom. 7: 24; 8: 2–4); so that we too can say with Paul, "I thank God through Jesus Christ our Lord", for "Christ is the end of the law for righteousness to every one that believeth".

14

IT would be good, at this juncture, to underline the danger of constant condemnation through the law, of which warning is given in Rom. 8: 1. It is probably the most prevalent cause of unhappiness and ineffectiveness among God's people. If the thunders of the law have ceased to terrify us through the peace of justification, the pointing finger of the law at our daily shortcomings is a constant discomfort. For we do "come short of the glory of God", and do so daily. What are we to do about it? We can liken ourselves, our renewed selves in Christ, to a piece of elastic. We are hidden in Him, we abide in Him, but Satan and his unclean demons, using all methods of allurement and disturbance that this distorted world affords, find plenty of means of pulling at the elastic! We are "drawn away of our own desires and enticed", and often the enticement leads on to consent, and we have sinned (James 1: 14, 15). Not the blatant sins of our past life, not certainly persistent sinning, for those who do that are not born of God (1 John 3: 9); but wrong attitudes of heart and mind, the quick word, selfishness, impatience, sins of the eyes, sloth in witness, the finer points of failure in holiness, which we had never even noticed in our insensitive days; these we fall into and mourn our fall. And the moment we have been spotted by the flesh, if we don't get clear at once, the law is in operation and we are condemned; for we have slipped back into that self-law-sin realm of Rom. 7.

Then how get out, and how learn to get out quickly? First, there is the big lie of the Accuser of the brethren. He will cast doubts on our crucified position in Christ, and try to tell us that our "old man" is still very much alive in us. That is a falsehood. But many accept it, and drag their feet through life on the false assumption that they have a divided self, a divided heart, a divided nature. Their conception of Christian living is a continuous struggle, a losing battle between their old nature and their new: "the flesh lusteth against the spirit, the spirit against the flesh; these are contrary the one to the other: so that ye cannot do the things that ye would". But that does not mean two co-equal natures battling in the believer one against the other. We have only one nature at a time; we cannot have more, for our nature is our very selves. We *were* by nature the children of wrath, we *are* partakers of the divine nature. That is the death and resurrection in Christ. No half measures about that! The old nature is the old man which has been crucified with Christ. The new nature is the new man, which is we risen with Christ and Christ living in us. This verse of Gal. 5: 17 on flesh and (the human redeemed) spirit is a concentration in a few words of the teaching of Rom. 7.

We live and walk in the Spirit, led by the Spirit (Gal. 5: 25, 16, 18). We are not then walking in the flesh (independent self), which we have crucified (5: 24). Because we are not walking in the flesh, the law has no claim on us, for it only presents its demands to independent self (5: 18). Because the law has no hold on us, the lusts of the flesh (the motions of sin in the flesh) are not stimulated by its challenge to impose their demands on us (flesh lusting against spirit), and to dominate our helpless self (ye cannot do the things that ye would). While we abide in Christ, we are dead in Him to law, and therefore dead to sin which is by the law.

But if we do not walk in the Spirit, then we return again under law, into the flesh and self-effort, and therefore under the dominion of sin in the flesh. That is not a question of an old and new nature, which was settled at the new birth. This "flesh and spirit" matter is a question of the daily walk, and the possibility of slipping back any time for a visit to the flesh and thus to sin, law and condemnation.

So we have to learn not to accept the big lie of our return to a permanent old condition, just because we are caught out by the flesh on occasions: nor to live in the bondage of a false, but very commonly held conception of being two people at once, with a civil war within, a good and bad nature, and who will win? No. Let us confess with the same assured voice as Paul that "the law of the Spirit of life in Christ Jesus hath set me free from the law of sin and death".

But then equally we must not stay, even temporarily, under condemnation, when Satan has caught us out. It is the easiest thing to do, and our distressed feelings are really self-pity and pride. It is not so much that we have grieved *the Lord* that disturbs us, as that *we* have failed. The acceptance of condemnation is a form of self-righteousness. *God* has told us, when we sin, to get quickly to the light, recognize and confess the sin, and then He is faithful and just to forgive us our sins, and to cleanse our consciences from all sense of unrighteousness. "The cleansing fount I see, I see; I plunge, and oh, it cleanseth me." To remain in condemnation, therefore, is really disobedience and hurt self. We can learn many lessons from simple believers who keep short accounts with

God. They are tripped up, they humbly recognize it, they claim the cleansing blood, and go on their way rejoicing; and often they use their testimony to such daily simple experiences to be a blessing to others. The elastic of the new self has been stretched by temptation; let it snap back into place.

15

W E have been looking together at this "mystery hid from ages and generations, but now made manifest—which is Christ in you"; but we have said nothing, except by implication, of the one way, the one Bible way, of experiencing this union with Him. Nothing could be simpler, of course it could not, because we were created to live like that, by the exercise of the one simplest of all human functions. It is the faculty of reception, called in the Bible—faith. "To as many as *received* Him, to them gave He power to become the sons of God, even to them that *believe* on His Name"; for believing is receiving. "*Received* ye the Spirit by the words of the law, or by the hearing of *faith*?"

We have pointed out all along that the one capacity with which human beings are endowed is that of receiving. The Creator gives, the creature receives. And obviously nothing is easier or more automatic than its constant exercise. Food, air, knowledge, the stored riches of this world, nothing is ours except by receiving it. "What hast thou that thou hast not received?" asked the apostle of the Corinthians.

There is only one law of receiving—the law of desire. Out of the limitless stores of this world's treasures, material, aesthetic, intellectual, yes and spiritual, we receive what we see to be available and want. He the Giver

of all, and we the recipients of what we *want*. The myriad
acts of reception and utilization in our daily lives are as
near as can be automatic, so soon as we want these things.
They are to our hands—the air we breathe, the food we
eat, the books we read; "for what we are about to *receive*,
may the Lord make us truly thankful", we pray at meals.

And Bible faith is as simple as that. That was one reason
why Jesus likened Himself to the simplest necessities of
life, which we take as we need without thinking: "I am the
bread of life"; "I am the light of the world"; "the water
that I shall give him. . . ."

But the one condition is always present—need: that is
desire, thirst, hunger. Hungry? Here's the food! Help
yourself! And that is why the first approach that God
makes to us in grace is the law; and the first work of the
Spirit is to convince the world of sin; and the first gift of
the gospel is repentance. We must be brought to see our
need, then His supply—and then the almost automatic
act of faith. "Why," we just cry, "He's ours. He died for
me. I'm forgiven! God's my Father and heaven's my
home." And I hardly realize that in fact I've received by
faith! Where there is the hunger, and where there is the
bread, we just find ourselves eating!

All the activities of life, material or spiritual, are
activities of faith—"faith which worketh by love", faith
stimulated into action by desire. We are justified by faith
(Rom. 5: 1). We are saved by faith (Eph. 2: 8). We are
sanctified by faith (Acts 26: 18); we receive and exercise
the gifts of the Spirit by faith (Rom. 12: 3, 6); Christ
dwells in our hearts by faith (Eph. 3: 17); we live by faith
(Gal. 3: 11); we walk by faith (2 Cor. 5: 7); we fight the
good fight of faith (1 Tim. 6: 12), and a dozen others.
And in every case it is the same process: need, recognition, reception, realization.

Supposing we have been justified by faith, what has taken place? My faith had been deprived of its old treasured possession—my own righteousness. The vacuum must be filled. How can a sinner be righteous before God? The *need* had been created. I was hungry and thirsty for righteousness. The word of God came, offering justification by faith in Christ. Hungry, needy faith recognized this Bible-attested fact, and almost automatically *received* it. To receive a thing is to *realize* that it is mine: "he that believeth hath the witness in himself". "Being justified by faith, we have peace with God." Need, recognition, reception, realization.

Now take it further. The justified are sanctified. Jesus, who is our justification in heaven, is our sanctification on earth. In Him we died. In Him we rose to newness of life, with Him as our life: "Christ liveth in me". How do we *know* this? By faith: by need, recognition, reception, realization. But let us remember faith is possession, and possession *is* realization. That this is not so easy is pictured for us in Heb. 3 and 4. Jesus is seen as our Moses and Joshua leading us through the wilderness and across the Jordan, testing us by many a strange privation and frustration, and exposing by that means the folly of judging by appearances, of the reactions of the murmuring self, of the sin of unbelief; and at the same time demonstrating in Moses the glorious deliverances of faith. Gradually the lessons are learned by the few, learned the hard way: the final crossing of faith is made through the Jordan, and the promised land reached. And this is interpreted for us as God's rest, present-tense rest, for the believer. It is made plain that they who believe "do enter into rest", as an actual and continual experience; and that this rest is not from working the works of God, but from working our own works. It is the rest-in-experience from independent self (4: 10); it is the replacement of ourselves by Himself, the Divine Worker. whose work is also His rest, for His yoke is easy and His burden light. But the writer to the Hebrews does not portray the entering in as a light matter. He says it is preceded by a severe operation, by the surgeon's knife of the Word of God which alone can penetrate to the innermost lair of the independent self, the "good" self, the Rom. 7 self, and expose the subtle difference between soul (independent self-activity) and spirit the dependent self) made one with God's Spirit, and thus between self-activity and the works of the Spirit. And he warns us to fear lest we miss it and seek earnestly to find it.

So in this next grade of faith for sanctification, as in the first for justification, there has to be the preliminary breaking up of the fallow ground, before the seed of faith can be sown and fructify. We saw in justification that the Spirit must cut faith free from its false moorings in righteousness by works, before it can set sail in the winds of the Spirit for its true haven in Christ. And that loosening process, the conviction of sin till the soul is desperate for salvation, often takes a long time and may involve drastic dealings. Only when there is the hunger and thirst of a faith in a vacuum can there be the simple reception and enjoyment of saving grace. And the same in sanctification. It is not now a question of the outward sins which subject the sinner to the wrath of God, but the indwelling sin which enslaves the saint; and once again faith has to be loosed from its false moorings. The saint has to learn that even in his new nature, self is as powerless as in the old; and that faith in any vestige of his own efforts to keep the law or work the works of God is like leaning his hand on a broken reed: it will pierce him; for law and sin are confederates in exposing the helplessness of self. Only by the hard way will he learn through wilderness privations and frustrations that faith, once more in a vacuum, must desperately seek another resting place; and only then can his eyes be opened to the inner meaning of these great truths we have been gazing upon. Then need is lost sight of in the recognition of the secret of supply; recognition is followed by glad reception, and reception by realization. "We which have believed do enter into rest."

Does that then mean that the hungry soul can do nothing about it, because it may be necessary for him to go through a further period of preparation and testing? Indeed no. The digging up of the fallow ground is as much God's business, His work of grace, as is the sowing and fructifying of the seed of faith. All we are told to do is to believe. Let us then do so boldly. The process of faith as presented to us in Rom. 10 is that it starts with the declared word of God (10: 17): "faith coming by hearing, and hearing by the word of God". That has already been given us in its completeness in the Bible, as it points to the living Word. The whole is open to us for our examination and digestion. But what actually happens, as we read it, is that out of its massed riches we "hear" certain truths by the Spirit, others we don't as yet "hear". Hearing is the operative word in this text, twice repeated. Hearing, it says, comes first by the Word of God. Some special words or truths are lit up to our hearts by the Spirit; we have been confronted just at that point by the Living God. Hearing then gives birth to faith. In other words, the Spirit creates hunger by the engrafted word, and faith, the receptive faculty now quickened into action, feeds on it. That will be first of all an inner reception; but Paul also says that the word of God from His mouth must become the word of faith in ours (10: 8, 9). We confirm the inner fact of our reception by the outer testimony with our lips.

We "confess with our mouths the Lord Jesus", and thus objectify to ourselves that He is in us what He says He is, and enable the Spirit to bear witness to it with our spirits.

So this we must do just up to the light we have, and that light will not be some passing impression from a message we hear, but something which shines deep into our hearts. Where God *shows* us truth, there enter in by faith.

In this matter of sanctification, what have you "seen"? Have you "seen" Gal. 2: 20: "I am crucified with Christ: nevertheless I live; yet not I, but Christ liveth in me"? Has light maybe dawned on you as you have read these pages? If so, receive as *fact* what God has shown to your heart. That is faith. Then confirm it by confessing with your mouth what you have received. You *may* at once have the realization of possession; or you may not. I personally did not for some time after I first saw the light on this. But, if *God* has given you the light and the gift of faith to receive, then, though you may be forgetful at times, or unbelieving at others, He will bring you back to your act of faith again and again; and *in His own time and way* you will come to have the witness in yourself, you will *know*. Don't try to work anything up. The consummation of your faith in assurance comes down from above just as much as the beginning of your faith—from the Author and Finisher of our faith.

16 THE GIFTS OF THE SPIRIT

BUT sanctification is only another grade of faith, and only a preliminary one at that. We go on to a life of faith with its many ramifications. We can only touch on one or two.

There is enduement for service. It is plain that when Jesus was leaving His disciples, it was that aspect of the coming of the Holy Spirit that He specially emphasized. "Ye shall receive power after that the Holy Ghost is come upon you." In the various epistles the Holy Spirit is revealed as the Giver of very many different gifts to the members of the body, so many and varied that they seem in general to cover all types of Christian activity. It is also said that *every* member of the body, if he is in the body, has been baptized into it by the One Spirit, has been made to drink of the same Spirit, and that "manifestations of the Spirit" have been given to "every man to profit withal" (1 Cor. 12: 7, 13). Such statements make it plain that every member of Christ's body has been baptized of the Spirit, and in being so, has received one or more of a great number of gifts. One list of these gifts is in Eph. 4: 11 for the up-building of the church: apostles, prophets, evangelists, pastors, teachers. These are the equipment of the Spirit for those called to leadership in the churches, though not exclusively for them. Other large and varied lists of gifts of the Spirit to all members of the body are mentioned

both by Paul and Peter in 1 Cor. 12: 8–10, 28–30; Rom.
12: 3–8; 1 Pet. 4: 10, 11. These include the gifts for both
spiritual and practical ministry, and for both natural and
supernatural activities. Twenty different gifts or ministries
are named. Some are in such normal use among believers
that even those who have them sometimes fail to realize
that they are precious gifts of the Spirit, and are just as
important to God and the church as the more "spiritual"
or spectacular ones: serving, helping, organizing (ruling);
leadership, hospitality, showing mercy, are all in the list;
and the thousands who exercise them are all the privileged
possessors of heavenly gifts; it is the Giver Himself living
His life through them. That one comprehensive gift
almost casually slipped into the 1 Cor. 12: 28 list—"helps"
—covers every kind of what we please to call "humble"
service for Christ.

Then there are the gifts of obvious spiritual ministry to
the body, already referred to: wisdom, knowledge, faith,
exhortation, prophecy, teaching, pastoral ability. Finally,
and most controversially, there are the supernatural gifts,
in the sense that by them the Spirit, though working as
usual through human agency, manifests Himself in ways
which appear superhuman. These are gifts of healing,
working of miracles, divers kinds of tongues, prophecy
(when regarded not as plain preaching, but as directly
inspired utterances), and discerning of spirits.

We need to spend a little time on these particular last-
named gifts, before getting back to the main line of our
consideration, the enduement of the Spirit, because the
exercise of the supernatural gifts has come right to the
fore in the last half-century and has spread world wide
through the church of Christ; and no earnest seeker after
God can fail to meet, some time or other, with the question,
What is my attitude to be toward those gifts? Are they for

me? And what is my attitude to be toward the many thousands who have received and exercise them?

First, then, there are the great numbers who claim outright that the most controversial, strange and startling gift of all, tongues, is the essential and only genuine evidence of receiving the baptism of the Holy Ghost. They base this claim on the plain evidence that regeneration of the Spirit in the early church was often accompanied by this gift. It was so at Pentecost, although nothing like that has ever been repeated, when visible tongues of fire rested on them and 120 spoke miraculously in 16 languages; quite obviously He does not come to-day on companies of believers in that way, not even on those who claim that speaking with tongues is the necessary evidence. But He also came with this gift on the first Gentile company of believers in the household of Cornelius; also on "certain disciples" at Ephesus, when first pointed to Jesus. It is also significant that others had received this gift whose conversions are recorded in the Acts, but no mention was there made of this fact, which gives ground for believing that the gift was widespread and common in the New Testament church. Paul is one instance of this, who "spake with tongues more than ye all", and the Corinthian church another. However, when all this has been stated, the fact remains that there is no Bible authority for saying that one gift of the Spirit, among many, is the essential evidence of His anointing, and we must reject that claim.

But, on the other hand, we must avoid the other extreme, very common among evangelicals, of rejecting the gift of tongues in our day either as an anachronism or as spurious. What right have we to say, with many, that it was a gift for that day, but not for ours? Certainly no Biblical authority. If some quote "tongues shall cease"

(1 Cor. 13: 8), so also at the same time shall knowledge! And if doubts are cast on the genuineness of the gift, we are given Biblical tests, of fruit (Matt. 7: 15-19), and confession of faith (1 John 4: 1-3). Thousands who do exercise this gift can pass both these tests, although there are always, as in all branches of the visible church, also the vessels unto dishonour.

What conclusion, then, do we come to? We trust to a balanced, middle-of-the-line one. I have personally never been honoured with this gift of the Spirit, so it is possible that I speak with more reserve than I should if I had been so blessed. Nobody who has mingled, as I have, with many who have received it, can doubt that it has brought outstanding, even transforming blessing to them. Many will say that they never felt they had received the true heart satisfaction they longed for until God met them in this way, nor the spirit of worship, nor full liberation to testify and pray. It is not for us to gainsay multitudes of testimonies of this kind.

Mature recipients of this gift, however, will also emphasize that it has its real dangers and possibilities of excess. This also is plain from Scripture in the Corinthian letter. They will point out that the gifts of the Spirit are different from the fruit, and that it is awfully possible to exercise even this holy gift in the flesh, where "the sanctification of the Spirit" has not accompanied it. Further even than that, just because in the exercise of this gift, some of the normal controls of the body are surrendered to the Spirit, it is possible, according to 1 John 4, for an evil spirit to enter, and it is a warning to remember that "tongues" is not a phenomenon peculiar to the Christian faith. It is exercised, under devilish control, in pagan cults, and in the non-Christian religions. A particular attraction also, in the reception of this gift, is its evident emotional effect; joy, praise, release, vocal expression are very evident, and that makes it unusually appealing to many; it stirs the emotional part of us, it satisfies and gives rein to feeling. While being in reality a spiritual emotion, it gives the appearance of a soulish one, and therefore, if we do not heed the word which divides asunder between soul and spirit, we may give ourselves to seek an emotion as an end in itself, and follow after tongues under the impression that to have that is to have HIM.

Let us now summarize our findings and see where they lead us. First, there is no Scriptural authority for the claim that to speak in tongues is the necessary evidence of receiving the Holy Ghost. But second, the gift of tongues was evidently common in the early church. Third, the large majority of those who have this gift to-day, testify to the blessing received from it. Fourth, there are unusual dangers attached to it, as evidenced by the warnings rather than encouragement given by Paul to those who exercise it. We must, therefore, honour those who have received this gift from God, and respect and be thankful for their testimony to its effects on them and in their witness; but at the same time we must be firm in our stand on our Scriptural foundations—that the Holy Ghost, God the Spirit, is in all regenerated believers, for He is the regeneration. He has come to reveal the Son in us as our justification, sanctification, and power for service. He in us is the Saviour, Sanctifier, Enduer with power from on high. He has reconciled us to the Father through His blood. He has nailed our old man to His cross, made us dead to law and sin, raised us up again with Himself as our life. He in us now manifests Himself to the world in saving grace through the varied gifts with which He has severally endowed us. Our part, and it is a real part, is to be conditioned by the Spirit to recognize, receive and realize what He is to us, in us, and by us. And that does not mean that we just "have it all in conversion", and that is all there is to it. No, there are definite grades of realization, of appropriation by faith, dependent on the preparatory work of the Spirit in bringing us by varied stages to see and feel our need. We have discussed these at length in relation to regeneration and sanctification.

We are now considering power for service, and the principle is exactly the same. We must first discover our need. The commonest way in which that happens is by many experiences of our hopeless inability to win others to Christ or to fulfil any spiritual ministry, and at the same time to be challenged by the way God uses others. Once again our faith has a vacuum. What is the secret of power, we ask. The answer is as before. "Christ the power of God". Christ "mighty in me toward the Gentiles", wrote Paul. Not without wrestlings was our faith brought to the simple receiving point for sanctification, and then to "the full assurance of faith". And not without heart-longings to the point of desperation will the revelation dawn on us: He *has* come; He *is* in us: "Go in this thy might"; "he that believeth on Me, out of his inmost part *shall* flow rivers of living water. This spake He of the Spirit." Make no mistake again: it has to be the word of God to oneself, not merely a general word of Scripture; it must be the engrafted word. We must come away from this dealing of God with us, whether it be in a crisis moment or over a period, with the solid knowledge that the Spirit of enduement for service is in us, as surely as the Spirit of regeneration and sanctification. Then only do we *know* Him within in this threefold manner. He may thus come as a rushing mighty wind with signs following; He may come, as He did to me, by a revelation of His own self

F

as the Executor of the Trinity. The point is that it is He Himself, and we know it is He.

The gifts are of His apportioning, who "divideth to every man severally as He will". We shall find that He will fit us into the type of life and ministry in which He expresses Himself through us by the gifts He gives us; and as we take our share in a living church fellowship, very often our brethren will see more clearly than we just where our gift lies. At any time God may pour out His Spirit on us in new ways. Let us put no limit on Him. We are told to "covet earnestly the best gifts", and to "desire spiritual gifts", so it is not out of place to look to Him for fresh enduements, just as those in the early church were filled and refilled with the Holy Ghost. Sudden discoveries are sometimes made, such as that one or another has an unexpected gift of healing or teaching or preaching. Let us expect the Lord to lead us on from waters to the ankles to waters to swim in. The gospel was preached in those early days "with mighty signs and wonders by the power of the Spirit of God", and "with divers miracles and gifts of the Holy Ghost", and should we not see the same to-day? The gift of healing, for instance, has been much revived in our day, services for "spiritual healing" are held in the churches of many denominations, and there are also great gospel and healing campaigns in many countries, including the mission fields. Once again they are subject to criticism, and there are the spurious as well as the genuine; it is also certainly true, whatever reason may be given, that many who go forward for healing do not receive it, or it does not last. But it is equally and undeniably true that God does heal to-day and that thousands can testify to it; also that many who go to these campaigns for the physical needs of their bodies return to their homes with the Saviour of their souls. And above all, there is plain ample warrant in the Scriptures for a healing ministry, both in the commands and promises of the Saviour, and in the practice of the early church, and personally I think we ought to be bolder in our services in offering healing for the sick in the name of Jesus, as well as salvation for the sinner.

17 THE DIALECTICAL PRINCIPLE IN ALL LIFE

MOVING on now into the problems of daily life, I want to underline the attitude of faith which unties every conceivable knot, and leaps over every high wall. It is really only a reiteration of what we have already seen, for faith is always just faith; but it concerns the problem of our divided outlook.

It is obvious that life is a mixture. As we have already seen, both good and evil are to be seen everywhere, in nature, in man, in politics, in industry. We never meet with one without the other: health—disease: prosperity—adversity: riches—poverty: love—hate: kindness—cruelty: life—death. We meet with these right in our personal lives; in our own hearts, in the family, in business, in church fellowship. Now it is human nature in us to want to embrace the one and flee from the other. But we can't solve life's problems that way. We can't escape the inescapable. Victorious living, indeed, means the ability to handle life's adversities as successfully, redemptively, and with as much understanding as life's prosperities. To do this, once again, we must go to the root of things. We must see all things as God sees them. It must be God looking through our eyes at our (His) problems, God thinking His thoughts in our minds concerning them, and God working in us to will and to do of His good pleasure.

Let us go back once again to the beginning. We have

our book of revelation—the whole Bible—so it is not difficult to trace the revealed mind and ways of God. He has not left us in bewilderment. His purpose and plan of grace is plain from Genesis to Revelation: all is centred in His Son. He was before all things, all was created by Him, and all is for His own pleasure (Rev. 4: 11). But He also foreknew the long, long trail to that final consummation, when He will gather together in one all things in Christ, in the new heavens and new earth wherein will dwell righteousness.

We have already seen that nothing exists without its opposite: to say yes to one thing is to say no to its opposite: to love one thing is to hate its opposite: light can only shine visibly in contrast to darkness: life "swallows up mortality". But when the Creator in His purpose of love and grace brought into existence His own "opposite", created beings in His own likeness, that their emptiness should be swallowed up by His fulness, their weakness manifest His strength, their darkness radiate His light, He foreknew and foresaw what might and did happen—that a great rift would appear in the harmony of His universe. As all negatives are the hidden, submissive partners to their positives, as the female to the male, as minors to majors, in the union of the two all life in thought and action being reproduced, so were we to be as the created to our Creator, as bride to Bridegroom, as servants to Master, as sons to Father. But as free selves, we could do what no other pair of opposites could do, we could refuse to keep this "first estate" of creature to Creator; we could aspire to be as God, the minor as the major, the darkness as light, the weakness as strength; and we could upset the equilibrium of our world. This is what God foresaw that we should do, and Lucifer and his angels before us. It meant the appearance of a whole principle of evil not in existence before, a negative that defied its positive and would replace it, a darkness that would be as light, an evil that would claim to be the good, a devil (and man) who would be God. The prophet boldly said of God that He "created evil" (Is. 45: 7), and it is true in the sense that a created being has the potentiality, the freedom to refuse to keep its own estate, and in refusing, to bring into manifestation the negative kingdom of evil as a power, "the power of darkness".

This was the warning God gave Adam and Eve: Beware of the tree of the knowledge of good *and evil*. Good they knew already, for all that God had created He pronounced to be "very good". The not-good (evil), the hidden opposite to good, was unknown to them. Let them beware: the existence of such an actuality as evil (in Lucifer and his hosts) was there before their eyes in the symbol of that tree. But into the trap they fell. No longer was the world within and without a world of pure goodness. Another spirit was working in them, the negative spirit of disobedience, infecting them as it infected all nature. There was not only the Yes of God's goodness around them, but the No of God's wrath on evil; and life had become a dichotomy, the clash of arms resounded through nature, the kingdom of light and the kingdom of darkness in mortal combat.

But both are still *God's* kingdoms, the kingdom of His Yes, the kingdom of His No; the kingdom of His grace, the kingdom of His wrath. We quickly begin to lose our way, if we are deluded into thinking that the foes in this war are of equal status. That never has been, nor could be. Major and minor, positive and negative, and so on down the line of all pairs of opposites, can never ultimately move from their created relationships, no matter how a satanic or human self may try to inflate itself from a nothing to a something. It is only bluff, self-deceit, false imagination, although it may and has caused all temporary upsets and discords in our world, and ends in an actual sphere of outer darkness for those who continue in it. No one has ever been on the throne of the universe but the perfect God Himself, perfect in foresight, perfect in plan and action, perfect in power, perfect in love.

Therefore to Him, and this is all-important to us, there never has been an unmanageable division, a dichotomy. He works all things after the counsel of His own will, *evil as well as good*. Evil serves His purposes as much as good. The devil is *His* agent.

The Bible makes it plain that, not only did He foresee the invasion of evil, but that He actively intervened to use it for His glory. Of us men in our evil ways it says that *He* hardens us (for we are all Pharaohs by nature), and is glorified in the hardening and its consequences (Rom. 9: 17): not indeed that He may destroy us, but that by making us sample the fruits of our rebellion, as many as possible of us may repent of our ways and be saved, for "He hath concluded us all in disobedience, *that* He may have mercy on all". Of the inanimate creation travailing in pain, we have already pointed out that it is *God Himself* who has subjected it to its present condition, not of its own volition, but in deliberate anticipation of the glorious deliverance to come (Rom. 8: 20). There is then this connection here, in the whole creation, between experience gained through suffering and subsequent glory, a lesson which we humans can learn intelligently and accept willingly. Good is faced with evil, and only by conquest of it becomes established goodness.

This is how God is establishing His eternal Kingdom which shall never be moved (Heb. 12: 28, 29). He Himself has planned and produced a creation which could and did go into reverse. It split wide open the positive goodness of all things and exposed the hidden opposite, bitter to sweet, lie to truth, hate to love, selfishness to unselfishness. And how did God meet this revolt? By Himself becoming the opposite to Himself—God becoming man, the Strong becoming the weak, Spirit taking flesh, and finally the Sinless becoming the sinner, Life becoming death. As captain (pioneer, trailcutter) of our salvation, He led the way by being perfected in the sufferings we suffer and by conquest of them. God tasted the duality of good and evil, tempted in all points as we are, yet without sin. But in being tempted he was totally victorious, in suffering His faith never failed, "faithful to Him that appointed him in all His house": and tasting the final form of evil, death for every man, He drank the cup to the dregs in the perfect obedience of faith, and thus destroyed in His resurrection him that had the power of death, that is the devil, and delivered his bondslaves from the fear of him. That is to say, He deliberately embraced evil, the worst evil Satan has it in his power to inflict. He permitted it to strike Him with all its force, and indeed to overcome Him in the flesh. He died at the hands of the evil one. But He died in the inner triumph of faith. This is revealed to us in Heb. 5, where we read that at Gethsemane He obeyed His Father to the limit, but in accepting the coming Calvary He first prevailed with Him by strong crying and tears that He should be saved out of death, "and was heard" because of His filial faith. By this means, by obedience and faith, He turned the evil back onto its perpetrator, and instead of being destroyed Himself, by His resurrection from the dead He destroyed the destroyer. He turned evil to good —by faith; and as the first pioneer on the road of salvation which we tread (Heb. 2: 10), He made a way of faith possible for all of us who will go through, believing Him in like "evil" circumstances. For us also, then, our evil will be our good. That is why in the same chapter, the writer says that the spiritually mature will, by going victoriously through life's experiences, learn to "discern both evil and good". When we are in spiritual infancy we judge things by outward appearances. If a situation is pleasant, it is good; if unpleasant, evil. But as we grow in the Spirit, we learn that all that comes to us is good if accepted in faith, and the only evil in the world for us is our inner unbelieving attitudes. Good and evil are not in our circumstances, but in ourselves, according to our reaction to them.

The Bible gives us classic examples of this. The most famous, of course, is Job. He was the outstanding man of faith of his generation, for God called him a "perfect and upright man", and God says that of no man unless his faith can be counted unto him for righteousness. But to him material prosperity was the obvious evidence of the favour of God. Then the tempests blew. Storm on storm swept over him. His faith bent beneath them, but never snapped. Some of the most glorious sayings of a faith under the cross were wrung from his tortured heart. He began in the fulness of faith: "The Lord gave, and the Lord hath taken away; blessed be the name of the Lord." But faith deteriorated, as always, through controversy, though still appearing in flashes through the thunder clouds: "Though He slay me, yet will I trust in Him": "I know that my Redeemer liveth, and that He shall stand at the latter day on the earth: and though after my skin worms destroy this body, yet in my flesh shall I see God": "When he hath tried me, I shall come forth like gold." It was a grim faith, an enduring rather than enjoying faith, magnificent, set by the Holy Ghost in James as the standard of endurance for believers of all time; but it lacked one transforming element: it was not an under-standing faith. He had to fight his way through blindfold. Perhaps he could have known earlier, if he had "broken" earlier. Who knows? It takes long enough for the Lord to break any of us, for we only break when we listen to His voice. The Lord spoke to Job in these closing scenes of the book, and gave him such a revelation of His majesty that Job was in the dust before Him; he had heard *of* Him before; now he saw Him. And what did he see? One who works all after the counsel of His own will, *evil* as well as good; for it was given to him to see and to record for us what lay behind his horrible trials—God using Satan, even stirring up Satan to bring external trials on Job so severe that all the watching hosts of heaven and all believers through history could learn the lesson: that God can implant such a faith and love for Himself in a fallen human that it transcends all that the world can offer and all that the devil can inflict (1 Pet. 1: 6–8). That revelation was of more value to Job and to us all than all the earthly blessings restored to him. There once for all is it recorded for us that Satan is still a servant of the Almighty—which is the very key to this problem of good and evil.

Joseph is another famous example. How far he clearly saw *God's* purposes through the years of shocking adver-sity, and equally through the first years of his fabulous prosperity, we do not know. We do know that he never lost the inner certainty that it was God who had given him those youthful dreams, for if he had, he never could, years after, have met the sudden challenge of the butler's and baker's perplexity over their dreams with the statement, "Do not interpretations belong to God? Tell *me* them, I pray you"; nor could he, two years later, have faced Pharaoh and his incredulous court in that dramatic scene, when Pharaoh told him that he had heard he was an interpreter of dreams, and without a moment's hesitation he answered, "It is not in me; God shall give Pharaoh an answer of peace." But certainly it all came clear to him when, in another moving moment, he saw his ten brethren standing before him, and "remembered the dreams which he dreamed of them", and later quelled their guilty fear by exclaiming, "Be not angry with yourselves, that ye sold me hither; for God did send me before you to preserve life . . . God sent me before you to preserve you a posterity in the earth . . . so now it was not you that sent me hither, but God"; and once again when he was dying, "Fear not . . . as for you, ye thought evil against me; *but God meant it for good*."

Here is God's perfection, as we come out of the tunnel of our investigation. "The tree of knowledge of good and evil." The divided outlook. Life, instead of being one good whole, has fallen into two opposing parts; the pairs of opposites have become enemies instead of friends and partners. Therefore life in the human must always be a tension, a constant propounding of problems with no adequate solution, a constant oscillation between the pleasurable and the painful. But when we raise our sights from the human to the divine, the whole picture changes. All started with God, all ends with God, and there is only One with whom He has to do: from eternity to eternity all is centred in Christ. Therefore whatever intervenes in history, whether pleasant or unpleasant, must be caught up into the stream of His purposes of grace in Christ. If the devil appears on the scene, then the devil must be His agent. If the fall of man adds to the chaos, then we learn that He had already foreseen that and the fallen first Adam was to be only a type in reverse (Rom. 5: 14) of the last redeeming Adam. This same Christ would Himself embrace the consequences of sin, atone for it, conquer it, and then produce out of the wreckage of fallen humanity a new race of sons to occupy the highest position in the universe, to share the throne of Him who is made "higher than the heavens", better than the angels, seated at the right hand of the majesty on high, "the fulness of Him that filleth all in all". Evil, then, would be to Christ an agency for good; not that evil comes from God, or is anything but evil; but faith utilizes it for good, because faith understands that God reigns in the darkness as well as in the light (Ps. 139: 12), and that God fulfils His own purpose through adverse circumstances which expose to man his inability, and spur him on to the receiving faith which liberates God to work. Therefore adversities of all kinds are sent from God, purposed by God, each as it exactly suits our condition, that we may learn and re-learn that "when I am weak, then I am strong". Good and evil thus cease to be divided to the eye of faith; they are reunited by the alchemy of the cross and resurrection, where self-reactions have died, and the living Christ deliberately furthers His victorious and redemptive plans through the assaults of His enemies.

18   IMPERFECTION POINTS TO PERFECTION

Looking, then, from heaven downwards rather than earth upwards, and realizing that God has always been nothing but the God of perfection, working *all* things after the counsel of His own will, we can see the whole problem of our chaotic world from a totally different point of view. The fact that God foreknew Satan's and man's disobedience and the resulting chaos, and had prepared the perfect remedy for it before it ever happened, gives us our key. Judgment and punishment there had to be, but He only ever predestined One to feel the full weight of His wrath, His only begotten Son. For all mankind He had only one purpose, to restore them in His Son to their original predestined perfection, and with them the whole fallen creation.

All, therefore, that happens to man in his present fallen condition has its own definite purpose—not of judgment, but of restoration. Suffering and sorrow is the will of God in this sense, that disobedience must have its due penalties and consequences, or there could be no ethical or rational basis to God's government; but the purpose, in grace, is not penal, but redemptive. Imperfection in all forms is God's finger pointing to perfection. It makes a tremendous difference to our outlook and actions when we realize this, for we learn to recognize that weakness, shortages, failures, disappointments, all that is short of the ideal, which are in God's order for this age, are for one purpose only: as parables, as figures, as signposts, pointing to the hidden sufficiency: types pointing to prototypes. It is the dialectical relationship: if there are weaknesses, there is strength: if shortages, supply: if failures, success. Thus we read that Adam was "the figure of him that was to come" (Rom. 5: 14) —the first Adam, the failure, pointed to the necessity in God's purpose of perfection, of a last Adam, the fulfilment, and to the certainty that that Perfect One was already there in the invisible, ready to be revealed in due time.

In this same way all the earthly appearances of things are types and shadows; for in God, the Perfect One, the Creator, who could create nothing but perfection, it is obvious that all which falls short of perfection in our world is not in its original state, but has fallen from it, from sufficiency to lack, from health to disease, from order to disorder, and has to be restored. The ceremonial worship of the tabernacle is an example of this shadow-substance relationship; the pattern was already there in the invisible, given to Moses on the Mount, from which he made the earthly copy; the writer to the Hebrews called it the shadow of which the Christ-to-come was the substance. Jesus on earth saw all things in this light. Every earthly object was to Him the figure of its heavenly reality. Bread —the living bread: water . . . the living water: birth . . . the new birth: light . . . the light of the world: life . . . everlasting life. Human events and activities were all symbols to Him of eternal events and realities, and He used them as parables: the sower, the husbandman, the prodigal, the pearl, the mustard seed, sheep, coins, fish . . .

What practical application has this for our daily lives? An important one. Every human situation of need with which we are faced is a voice from God saying to us: "That points to My fulness: that imperfection to My per-

fection: that need to My supply: that perplexity to My
solution." The whole of life in its fallen state is a great
finger-post pointing the way from the imperfect human to
the perfect divine. But that would not be of much help if
we were left with pointing signposts and an impassable
gulf, only to be bridged in a future life. No. Jesus incarnate, crucified, resurrected and ascended has altered that.
Grace has already bridged the gulf: from heaven to earth
and back from earth to heaven. The result is that God
permits needs in our lives *that* He may *now* supply them
in Christ. That is the point. Needs, shortages, problems
are summonses to *faith*. That is why they are God's will.
They are His necessary way of compelling us flesh-bound
humans to recognize our earthly limitations, to be dis-
satisfied with them, to seek the way to transcend them, and
to become agents of redemptive faith. There He stands
just the other side of the barrier, beckoning to us and saying, "I am the answer, I am the supply. I have come to
you in Christ. Receive Me in this situation." For need is
a shadow. And what casts the shadow? The light. No light,
no shadow. The light of God's fulness shines on this
world. The oppositions of Satan, to which we add the sin
of unbelief, have interposed themselves and cast the
shadows of the lacks of this life. Christ has come to
destroy that intervening barrier. Then to those who believe
Him, it is no longer a barrier but a bluff—a challenge
to faith.

That may or may not mean that the actual material
situation is changed. Very often it is. But it means that we
look at all situations with God's eyes. We see that in
reality they are *His* situations, into which He has deliberately put us that He might be glorified in them. Therefore
before we call, He is already answering, because He Himself has instigated this actual situation with His answer all

prepared. Our calling is His stirring of us to feel the need and recognize that here is a situation in which God is going to do something. Our action then is to call on Him, in other words, to take the attitude of faith. Faith means that we turn our attention from the need to the Supplier who is already supplying that need, and who allowed the need because He intends to supply it to His glory. Therefore our calling on Him is our seeing Him and praising Him and confessing Him before men, and awaiting the manifestation of the supply.

Paul's thorn in the flesh is a perfect illustration of this. Though a "messenger of Satan", *God* sent it, for it was "given" him for a deliberate purpose—to keep him from the subtle inroads of self-esteem, leading to self-reliance. The trial was deep and prolonged (probably increasing blindness). At first he thought that the One who had done physical miracles in other bodies through him would do the same in him. But no. After three separate appeals, we may suppose with intervals between each, God's word came clear to him. He was to prove the power of God *in* his weakness, not *from* it; not by deliverance from it, but by constant ability to transcend it. The Supplier had met his need—this time as abounding spiritual supply overflowing an ever-present physical need. A seeking faith became a praising faith, and reaching out over all the unending trials and sufferings of his pioneer life, he gathered them up in one embrace of praise and thanks for all of them (2 Cor. 12: 10), and especially for the blessedness of that basic lesson for all time: "when I am weak, then am I strong".

And, far more important, when his own lesson had been well-learned, his testimony has transmitted the secret, even more clearly than Job himself, to millions of succeeding generations. Our trials are *God's* trials, *given* us for a purpose, exactly suited to us. Our lacks are *God's* lacks, our perplexities are *God's* perplexities. Before the trials, God has already prepared the deliverance and sends us the trials that He may manifest Himself through them. The trial is to stimulate faith, and faith is seeing Him who is invisible. As we do this, in praise and expectation, He gives the answer. It may or may not be the kind of deliverance we anticipate. But it *will* be what we can recognize and receive with joy as *His* answer, and to which we can testify. The need will have been wholly met by *His* supply in *His* way, and, as a pebble thrown into a pond, the widening circles of the testimony will do their redemptive work far beyond our knowledge.

G

19 HOW TO TURN EVIL INTO GOOD

W E give negatives positive names, as does the Bible, because they are real entities; but at the same time, as we have already said, by doing so we tend to obscure their real condition as negatives. Basically, evil is merely not-good: bitter is not-sweet: hate is not-love: man is not-God; and so on. And when we see all negatives in their true character, we see this vital fact —that they are merely the reverse side of their positives. They are not meant to be anything apart from their positives. They have no rightful existence except as minor to major, female to male, no to yes, each by union with its positive giving distinctive birth and form and character to some manifestation of its positive, as do the minor to the major keys in music. Therefore, insofar as they have been infected and inflamed by a contrary spirit and thus removed out of their proper place in the eternal economy of God, He who is the Positive, the All in all, must necessarily find means to restore them. This He has done in what the Bible calls "the reconciliation of all things" (Col. 1: 20; Rom. 8: 19–21). He will not finally permit any portion of His creation to remain "out of temperature": He "will gather together in one all things in Christ".

It is not, of course, material things which are to blame or which have gone wrong, except insofar as they share in "the corruption which is in the world through lust".

Things are but the servant of spirit; it is the negative spirit, free, intelligent, deliberate, which has done the damage.

We have already seen how God has effected this reconciliation through His Son, but we need to note not only the fact, but also the way in which He did it, for it is the only principle by which this contrary spirit can be dealt with throughout human history. First, in the natural He accepted vicariously all that comes to human beings in this distorted world, all the trials, privations, weaknesses that flesh is heir to, and all the persecutions right up to the final stroke the negative spirit of evil could deal him—the death on the cross. He was "crucified through weakness". In the natural he did not resist evil. He went further than that: He positively accepted evil as the predetermined *will* of the Father. He swallowed it in its most virulent forms. But what broke His body and agonized His soul, could not touch His spirit. There neither Satan nor the threats and deeds of cruel men, nor evil in any form, could get any footing. "The prince of this world cometh, but hath nothing *in* Me." In that inner sanctuary dwelt only the living God fulfilling His own reconciling purposes through the yieldedness, faith and obedience of the One who would walk the saving way. He was "put to death in the flesh, but quickened by the Spirit". That vicarious process by which, as the representative human, He first embraced all that the negative spirit has loaded upon humanity even unto death, but then was raised again by the Positive Spirit as the One whom death could not hold, meant death to that negative spirit in all who join themselves to Him by receptive faith. Through death, He destroyed (or literally, annulled) him that had the power of death, that is the devil, and delivered them who through fear of death were all their lifetime subject to bondage.

Released from the negative spirit, all negative conditions fall back into their rightful place for those in whom
Christ lives: the bitter brings out the flavour of the sweet,
light shines out of darkness, mortality is swallowed up by
life, evil is overcome by good. That is to say, what comes
to us in the natural as trial, sorrow, suffering, privation,
persecution, and we feel as such in our bodies and souls
and know the sharpness of them, in our spirits we see to
be, not objectionable invasions of something contrary and
frustrating, but the way in which we "bear about in our
body the dying of the Lord Jesus". He again is dying in
us (His human body) in all kinds of situations, and He is
rising victorious in us. His life is manifest to all in our
mortal flesh (in our visible enjoyment of the unenjoyable):
the integrating victory of the Spirit is seen in us as we
"take pleasure" in things which are the opposite to
natural pleasure—"infirmities, reproaches, necessities,
persecutions, distresses" (2 Cor. 12: 10); evil is servant to
good, hate the seedplot of love.

And inner integration in unpleasant situations has far
wider repercussions than the personal. It is the continua-
tion of Christ's vicarious sufferings and saving resurrection (Col. 1: 24). Christ still dies and rises again for the
world through His spiritual Body, as He did in His
earthly one. That does not mean that Christ's unique
redemptive work for the world was not completed or
could in any least degree be effected through any body
except His own, conceived by the Holy Ghost and born of
the Virgin Mary, the Jesus of history who was crucified at
an exact location, buried in a known tomb, and viewed in
His resurrection body by many witnesses. But it does
mean that the application of His triumph worldwide
through the succeeding centuries, in the gathering out of
a people to His Name, in the building of them up in their

most holy faith, is always and only by this one death and resurrection process, the *way* of the Cross, though not that one unique *work* of the Cross. It is constantly the Christ who lives in the believer walking in us the way of vicarious death and resurrection in every one of millions of situations and spheres of service, right along the line from the mother with her family, to the worker in his job, to the missionary on his field. The point so hard to learn and relearn in our Christian immaturity is God's way of the cross: confronted with the necessity of a world that must die to sin and rise to righteousness, the One who need not so die and rise went that way first Himself; and by that vicarious act released death and resurrection power through Himself for a world. "Death worketh in us, but life in you."

This is the way of the intercessor. Jesus "poured out His soul unto death", and so, it says, "made intercession for the transgressors" (Is. 53: 12). Because of that act of death-intercession, God poured His resurrection life both into the Saviour's dead body and through Him into all who receive Him. The fruit of His intercession was the life-giving Spirit sent into the world, saving to the uttermost them that come unto God by Him. And every life of fruitful service has this at its roots: the corn of wheat must die, if the world is to feed on its fruit. We say, "That person must change; that situation must alter." God says, "You change first, the other will follow." As one has said, "I don't like you: what's the matter with *me*?" The first death in a human situation in which I am involved is in me, in my natural reactions of resentment, condemnation, unbelief. Only when I am consciously "through" to resurrection ground, experienced in my heart by peace and praise and love, can divine life through me touch the situation. As this is true in every daily detail of life, in every domestic, business or church trial, so is it true in the mainstream of our life's ministry. All the great intercessors of the Bible were living sacrifices for the people for whom they interceded; they lived and died vicariously. Not that there is merit or power in the out-poured life of a human intercessor, but it is the Interced-ing Spirit in him which takes him this death way; He does that to involve him so completely and importunately in the pursuit of his intercession that the Spirit can speak by him the authoritative word of faith—God's "I will"; and that will be followed, as surely as harvest follows seedtime, by the intercession gained—the wonderful works of God. The patriarchs, Moses, Joshua, David, the disciples, Paul, and countless others through history, were all intercessors who gained their intercessions, serving their own generation in the will of God.

20 NEED IS THE EVIDENCE OF SUPPLY

THESE are the ways by which God makes the evil handmaid to the good, and conditions us for His grace. But he does it, not only by confronting us with the plain facts of the needs and corruption, the miseries and confusion of our fallen estate: He does it also by the chastisements and judgments which "must begin with the house of God".

Examples of these are obvious throughout the Scriptures. Against apostate Israel He sends an agent of the devil, yet calls him "Nebuchadnezzar, *My* servant". Israel is beguiled into the negative kingdom, "the power of darkness", and worships idols (not-gods) and does evil (not good) works; she must receive the just recompense of her false (not-true) way of life in misery (not-happiness), slavery (not-freedom), and corruption (not-purity), and learn her hard lesson. At other times the prophets speak of God sending on them His hornets, His army of destroyers (the locusts, caterpillars, etc.), His drought, the Assyrians, rod of His anger. But the prophets always also make clear that God sends them for redemptive, not punitive reasons. By these means Israel will learn, or some of them anyhow, to discern between the false and the true, and the devil's agents will be God's agents in directing the wanderer home with the prodigal's cry: "How many hired servants of my father's have bread enough and to spare, and I perish with hunger." Often we try to escape the issue by regarding chastisement and judgment as a "permissive will" of God, as if God was passively allowing the devil to have some of his way, or as if the consequences of disobedience were the outworking of an impersonal law. But the Bible never speaks of it like that. It speaks directly of God saying and doing things which the natural mind roundly condemns as impossible harshness and cruelty in a God who is love, and even the spiritual mind, which has not understanding on this point, will seek to excuse or sidestep. No. It is God, the God of mercy, who hardens the heart of the persistent sinner, who dulls the ear and blinds the eye of the disobedient. The same God who says yes to righteousness must say no to sin. It is God's inevitable dealings with nature in reverse. It is God's grace at work in reverse.

But it is God's grace. That is the important point. God, being positive love, positive life, positive goodness, can work in no other way than according to His own nature, in determined and unceasing works of grace. He must restore rebel negatives to their predestined estate of submission to their positives: He must overcome evil by good, clothe the corruptible with incorruption, and swallow up mortality in life. This He did, in His "determinate counsel and foreknowledge", by the One who died to that negative spirit in His death for all who receive Him; replaced it by His own positive Spirit in His resurrection; and in His ascension awaits the day when the last negative (death: not-life) will be put under His feet.

This means, then, that all the consequences of our wrong ways, which are His deliberate judgments on us, are determined acts of pure grace. They are to open our eyes, teach us our lesson of the goodness of God leading us to repentance, and then to give us the glorious revelation of a life which has already swallowed up death, a goodness which has overcome evil, a sweetness which has dissolved bitterness—in our Lord Jesus Christ. In other words, judgments are pointers to grace, signposts: and not to a grace which has to be sought somewhere or manufactured; but which was there long before the judgments, and the judgments are only the necessary way of getting the grace through to us, conditioning us to accept it.

Long before there was a condition of need God had completed His work of perfect creation. The fall and its consequences have been an apparently tragic interlude, but that was foreseen and provided for in "the Lamb without blemish and without spot; who verily was foreordained before the foundation of the world". Therefore, as we have already said, God has always had His fulness in readiness to replace our emptiness, His perfection our imperfections, His light our darkness, His life our death. He has always intended, planned and provided total supply for every human need, and the supply has always been there. It is not that our need initiates the demand for its supply and must somehow call the attention of the Father to it and persuade Him to supply. No indeed. HE initiated the need so that we might find all our supply already there in His and our Christ! The need is the proof that the supply is there, and is merely God's means of conditioning us to be agents of faith. It is God who confronts us with every kind of problem, inability, difficulty, that, in our weakness, He may flash the spark of faith into our hearts, His faith, that His supply for exactly that situation was there long before. "Eat, o friends; drink, yea drink abundantly, o beloved."

That is the meaning of parable, and all life is a parable, if we understand it; for a parable is an earthly representation of a heavenly fact. But what fact? It is the story of some human need picturing a spiritual need—the man who fell among thieves, the lost sheep, the prodigal son. But is that all? No, the story always points on to the supply of that need, the provision of grace, of the kingdom of heaven. Parables underline human need as pointers to the One who from eternity has been Supplier of all need. Parables, therefore, are signposts, not to the need which is obvious, but to the One who has brought the need to our attention because He intends to supply it. In this sense, the whole of our human existence is one continuous parable. It is one vast imperfection pointing to the invisible perfection already ours in Christ; one vast confusion pointing to the eternal order in Him. It stirs in all who have eyes to see the longing for that final perfection at His coming, but at the same time it is God's summons to us to receive by faith in the here and now the supplies of so many needs.

To repeat once more. Can we catch a glimpse of this truth and its effects on our whole outlook? All evil, sin, and their consequences are negatives which have got out of place and made their unlawful appearance in God's universe. The Bible gives them positive names because they are positive facts—the kingdom or power of darkness. But their basic reality is not positive; they are the negatives of their true positives which they have blatantly tried to dethrone and called themselves the positives: thus the creature is in reality the not-Creator, rebellion not-obedience, unbelief not-faith, pain not-pleasure, and so on. God, the eternal positive, the eternal yes, is in process of restoring all to their proper place, the negatives in rightful submission to and union with their positives, their interaction being the basis of the manifestation of the glory of God.

To bring about His eternal purpose, God gives us to

taste and know the bitter fruits of our false negatives by
His judgments on all that is the not-good, not-sweet, not-
loving, not-selfgiving, not-humble, in our lives, and in the
life of the church and the world; but He gives this not for
judgment, but to shut us up to His grace, to the salvation
and consequent restoration planned in Christ before the
false kingdom of negation was in existence. It was fulfilled
by Him when He gathered the great negation of humanity,
its not-rightness, into Himself on the cross and took it
into His death, and when He arose to be the first-born of
the new creation, where the positive and negative are
joined in eternal fruitfulness by the union of Christ and the
redeemed sinner. This fulfilment is in process of realization by the Spirit working in the world of men, and join-
ing the negatives to their one Positive. Wherever, therefore, the Spirit confronts us with the tragedy and destitu-
tion of the not-righteous (the sinners), having first confronted us with our own need, He does it with the express
purpose of saying to us with as loud a voice as possible:
"I am come to redeem these falsely opposing negatives
and rejoin them to their Positive: the not-righteous (the
sinner) to be clothed with righteousness: the not-full (the
empty) to be filled. I point out the false negatives to you,
just so that you should immediately combine with your
outlook which sees the negative, the not-full, not-happy,
not-righteous, not-true side of things, the positive outlook
of faith which sees ME present to fulfil all need; and the
fact that I have shown you the need is my assurance to
you that I have come with the supply already in My
hands. See Me, believe Me, co-operate with Me, and I
will work this work of salvation through the faith I put
into you, and your labours of love that go with it."

21

No subject is more discussed to-day than church unity. Ecumenicity, the union of the churches on a world basis, is considered by many to be the chief goal of Christendom in the twentieth century. But the Bible does not ask the question, Is the church divided? It asks, Is Christ divided? (1 Cor. 1: 13.) And the Bible does not recognize more than one church in actual existence! Are all denominations, then, a declension from the New Testament standard? Ought they all to be wiped out? By no means so. Variety is a sign of life, not death. The one church of Christ, explicit and implicit through the New Testament writings, is already subdivided in its pages into what we call local churches, "the church of Ephesus", "the church in Thyatira", "the church which is in his house". A denomination basically is merely a church or group of churches which has a name of its own; the word means that. It can be compared with the differentiation between the various species of the animal, tree or plant world, and the command given to Adam to name them.

No. We are in danger of moving in the wrong direction. Our objective is not to make one outward church by ironing out denominational differences, names or organizations. There never has been more than one church on earth since Pentecost. That is what the Bible teaches and the Holy Ghost recognizes. Christ *has* broken down all middle walls of partition and made in Himself "one new man", the church which is one body, but many members, "so also is Christ". Christ and His church are synonymous. The danger is not variety or continuance of many denominations, large, small, ripe in years or just being formed. Fresh fellowships in Christ, fresh in love, in zeal, with some Spirit-revealed emphasis of "the truth as it is in Jesus" which may have become overlaid in older groups, is the lifeblood of the growing church, just as we go to annual flower-shows to delight in the new varieties and combinations of blooms produced by modern horticultural methods. They are all the One Church, the only Church recognized in God's Word.

The problem is not in plenty of variety and the constant rebirth of the church in new forms and under new names; we are fools if we think we can stop that and time-wasters if we attempt it; men cannot stop the seeding of grace any more than of nature. The mistake on the one hand is to be occupied in uniting the outward church instead of affirming the permanent unity of the one inner church, and fostering all means of fellowship between those who hold the Bible faith once delivered to the saints: or, on the other hand, to be so provincial in outlook that, instead of seeing the one Christ in the one body worldwide and throughout the whole length of history, we see minute fragments of the church of history and almost call them *the* church, usually because they are the one fragment in which we have grown up or through which we have gained light. Without realizing it, maybe, we have then slipped into a dual loyalty to which we seek to give equal allegiance, and that is idolatry. Our loyalty is single, eternal, unchangeable—to a Christ who is Head and body complete.

We see Him in His one church, the fulness of Him that filleth all in all; it includes every redeemed person through history, and together we all form "the perfect man" in Christ. Let there be thousands of convenient ways of worship, forms of organization, special emphases of message and doctrine, affinities of fellowship, which form us into denominations or local churches; but loyalty to earthly forms is not of the same quality as loyalty to the heavenly Head and body, and comes under the category of other earthly loves and loyalties which Jesus said must even be hated (father, mother, wife, children), if they shew signs of being rivals to the One.

True ecumenicity, therefore, sees with utmost clarity the fact of the one church of the redeemed joined to the Redeemer, and basically recognizes no other. But being human, and living in the localized and organized communities in which alone humanity can function, there is the true place for the local church fellowships; and these, as they expand and become linked by community of conviction, form world organizations—denominations. There can be any number of these and no limit to their increase if they remain faithful to their one foundation; and a truly ecumenical outlook will both recognize and encourage this, because its eye is always fixed on the one Head and body, and the rightful human variety in the body, which "also is Christ". It may rightly endeavour to encourage co-operation and deeper mutual love and understanding between denominations large and small, and corporate witness and activities; but it will not seek to dissolve or fuse any into an organized unity unless there is clear leading among the members. The whole history of the church of Christ in the vigour of its expansion has been by fission rather than fusion. The birth of the church was out from Judaism, and the great movements of the Spirit through the centuries have been dynamic outbursts which could seldom be retained in the existing organizations. If that has been so up to the present, we are foolish if we think the pattern will now change. It is really a form of unrecognized pride when the present-day large denominations, which were themselves small, persecuted, and despised schismatics in the view of the established churches of their day, now in their era of consolidation point an equally contemptuous or critical finger at new movements, and perhaps speak of them as "the sects" or even "the fringe sects", or "the lunatic fringe", or "the religious underworld".

Opposition to the start of new movements is natural on the part of the older ones, who may be losing members and who will not be seeing eye to eye with the newer brethren in the reasons for their new start. It is just here that the single eye is tested out. Can we feel the human hurt of such losses, yet squarely recognize that the church is always and for ever one, and that no minor differences affect that? Can we act as one, and find means to bridge in fellowship a parting in organization? There are often those who leave their church fellowship for unworthy reasons; there are others who should hold on in charity and faithfulness, in the hope of being channels of blessing in parched soil; and there is always the tendency to regard a new and vital movement as sheepstealers, whether deliberately or not; but none of these sore spots justify any deviation on the part of the newer or older churches from the fundamental fact of the one and only church of Christ, and from carefully guarding against more than a minor loyalty to any earthly section of it. The older must beware of resentment, and the younger of the "I am holier than thou" attitude.

The revelation of the One Church, given in its completeness in Ephesians, is basically recognized by most born-again people; but the fellowship is mostly only on a believer-to-believer level. Much fewer have come to see the One Church on a church level, and as a church fellowship make more of their membership in *the* church than in their local affiliations; to do this probably necessitates a toning-down or elimination of emphasis on local membership. There are vigorous movements of the Spirit to-day with many local churches, which have no membership, in order to underline the unity of the one body. The ecumenical movement of to-day, with its zeal for external unity, gives to the world the false impression of the non-existence of the real unity which in fact is and has been since Pentecost, and the wrong idea that variety in the churches on earth is an evil rather than a good thing.

Fellowship, therefore, rather than individualism does need emphasizing as the pattern for the believer. We do not live merely on a vertical plane, but also on a horizontal. All our vertical relationships of faith in God through Christ are consummated by our horizontal relationships with each other: "that ye also may have fellowship with us: and truly our fellowship is with the Father and with His Son, Jesus Christ." One does not properly function without the other. This was plain in the early church, when their meetings were on the free sharing basis. We see them in their normal condition when Paul was checking the Corinthians for over-enthusiasm: "How is it then, brethren? When ye come together, everyone of you hath a psalm, a doctrine . . ." Evidently the flow of the Spirit through the members of the body was such a normal experience that he had to urge them to quieten down a bit. This was horizontal fellowship; and we have to face the fact that the churches through the centuries

have so changed their character that such a flow of fellowship is very much the exception as the regular characteristic of a church at worship.

The one-man ministry, which is almost universal to-
day, results in the Lord's people meeting to be ministered
unto, rather than to minister to the Lord and each other.
It appears that the pattern of the early church was the
Spirit manifesting the gifts through the members as He
pleased. Those who had gifts suitable for responsibility in
the church were then set apart as elders and deacons, and
used their gifts under the control of the Spirit, leaving
room at the same time for free expression by all the
members. What we wrongly speak of as "coming to
church" (for the church in the New Testament was
always people, not a building), was referred to by the
apostle as being for the purpose of "exhorting one
another" (Heb. 10: 25; cf. 3: 13).

One church—yes. Local church fellowships, yet part of
the one church—yes. But the church does not exist for
itself but for those outside of it. A church which is not a
propagating church is a swamp, not a river. It *must* witness
or die. Those Roman Catholic worker-priests in Paris,
Abbé Godin and the others, who were later suppressed by
the hierarchy, were appalled at the way the average
Roman church functioned as a feather-bed for the faithful,
while the mass of Parisians around them were totally
indifferent to any religion. The same may be said of us
Protestants. A church of the Holy Spirit, who came to
point the world to Christ, cannot rest without finding
means of reaching its neighbourhood. That is the spear-
point of its fellowship life. We know of churches on the
mission fields which in their zeal to reach the outsider
give up the use of their church buildings for certain weeks
each month on the Lord's day, and go to hold their

H

services in neighbouring towns, in order to reach the unchurched.

That again is the dire danger of a one-man ministry. How easy for the "layman" to say, "Why should I do his job for him?" How can the "laity" (a word which in itself shows how far we have drifted from the pattern of the New Testament Ecclesia), be retaught that *they* are the church, and the minister, if they have any, but one of themselves? The whole church in action—a royal priesthood—that is the New Testament norm. The means must vary. It is the job of a witnessing fellowship, right with God, right with each other, with something vital to give to the have-nots around them, to find God's ways of corporate evangelism. The fellowship becomes an army, the neighbourhood its battlefield.

But no living church remains a local church. The Saviour who gave His first Jerusalem church a worldwide commission, gives it to all: "To every creature . . ." What daring! What a comprehensiveness! To *every* creature. It stirs the blood of anyone with a particle of vision. We have *the* Saviour. But He is the *world's* Saviour, and there is none other. Our church, our assembly, has a debt to pay. The fact that we belong to one human family afflicted with one mortal disease, and that we have been given the only remedy, puts us under an inescapable obligation to share our secret. Antioch sent forth her Paul and Barnabas, Berea her Sopater, Thessalonica her Aristarchus and Secundus, Derbe her Gaius, Lystra her Timothy. Whom do we send forth? Where are we reproducing ourselves? In Africa? India? Latin America? The Far East?

22   LOVE IN ACTION

THE circle is now completed. From God to God. Jesus the author *and* finisher of our faith, the beginning *and* ending, the Alpha *and* Omega. All is circular. God went out from Himself in creation, only to return to Himself, as He gathers together in one all things in Christ, when the "Son Himself shall be subject unto Him, that God may be all in all". Prayer is the same, and faith the same. Each proceeds from God who is working all things after the counsel of His own will. It is He that puts us in situations in which He can arouse in us a sense of need expressed in prayer, and quicken in us the assurance of supply expressed in faith. It is God's intercession and God's believing, consummated in God's appearing in a situation, reconciling some part of His lost creation to Himself. We commonly call it our work of intercession, or service to Christ. But it is not that. It is God in action, love in action, God reconciling the world to Himself by us. He is the intercessor who stands in the gap, but doing it "by the hand of" His servant David or Moses or any of us. The divine imperative that impels us is His. The vicarious sacrifices by which I take the place of those for whom I intercede are His. The faith which "commands" the deliverances is His. The spirit of a person expresses itself through the activities of soul and body; so also the Divine Spirit expresses Himself by us, the Body of Christ.

God is love. Love is a permanent debtor to all, the servant of all. That is love's nature. Can God live in me and not love? That profoundest passage ever written on love by the apostle of love—1 John 4: 7–21—takes us to the one source. We must love, we do love, let us love, because if we are born of God, we are born of love, we have a new love-nature. The ever invisible God is only made visible when we love. Here is God incarnate again. And if our confession of faith is the indication that He dwells in us, then we are world-lovers, for "the Father sent the Son to be the Saviour of the world".

Can there be passivity in us then, or merely spiritual self-interest? A contradiction in terms! God is an outgoing God, for love is outgoing. God is self-giving, for love is self-giving. Then so are we (1 John 4: 17). Freedom from self is freedom to love. There is no other freedom. God only is free, because God is love. Service is freedom. Sacrifice is freedom. Self-denial is freedom; that is why Paul warned us not to use our liberty "as an occasion to the flesh", for that would mean immediate bondage again: "but by love serve one another". We are a people with a purpose, for we are people of love. Love is dynamic, love is unresting, love is action.

But there is a law of love—a principle—that royal, that kingly law of Scripture. Not in our love service, any more than in the other grades of spiritual life, can we go any way about it but one. Once again we have to get a clear grasp of the interaction in service between the redeemed human spirit and the divine indwelling Spirit. We examined that same delicate balance in the daily life of the believer, the relationship so perfectly presented in the "nevertheless I live", and the "yet not I, but Christ liveth in me" of Gal. 2: 20. We saw that while we are still on earth, we still have a distinct dual consciousness which cannot be transcended: we are continually conscious of ourselves in all our reactions to our daily environment: we are also Christ-conscious, both by a constant subconscious sense of His presence within, and by the conscious contacts of faith, as we directly relate ourselves with Him on numberless occasions. We have to await the final resurrection of the body to experience a permanent unification, where there is no further division between the renewed self and the Indwelling Self.

We saw that the reason for this is that we are still members of a fallen humanity, and a fallen humanity means a humanity separated from God. The fall, separating the self in false independence from the eternal Self of God, gave humanity its name of shame—the flesh. Flesh is helpless humanity in its conscious separation from the One who alone is its help and strength: and being helpless by nature, if it is not abiding in Him, it is at once subject to its own instincts and appetites, a self-loving flesh. Even the Saviour Himself, as we have seen, had to be in the flesh if He was to identify Himself with humanity. But in His case it was "in the likeness of sinful flesh", not in actual sinful flesh: that is to say, as being in the flesh, He was conscious of being a human self distinct from the One who indwelt Him. But he so continuously abode in the Father, and lived and spoke by Him, that there was never one moment in which the instincts or appetites of the flesh could dominate Him, and thus the egoistic spirit of Satan enter Him. The flesh of the Saviour was real flesh, conscious of a human selfhood apart from the Father within, necessitating a constant series of obediences in the flesh throughout His human life (Heb. 5: 8), a choosing of the divine will against the natural human shrinkings of a human will, but never descending to the disobedience and rebellion of fallen humanity.

The fact, then, that we have to realize and never forget is that humanity in this alien world with its divided knowledge of good and evil, even if it is redeemed humanity, not the old man in Satan, but the new man in Christ, is still *flesh*: that is to say, we shall always be conscious of ourselves as distinct from the indwelling Other Self—Christ: we shall always, as Paul says, walk in the flesh, though not war after it. And because we are flesh we are always conscious of our innate weakness, insufficiency, inability. It is not wrong to feel like that, for that is all human nature can ever be, for it is all that it was created to be. But it does mean—and here is the point of supreme importance—that every summons to us by our indwelling Lord, to action, to service, to witness, to love, meets immediately with a reaction from our self-conscious selves of "I can't", "I fear to", "That is impossible", "Who is sufficient for these things?", and so forth. The first reaction of our renewed selves is opposition to the call! That does not mean that it is wrong for us to have such a reaction. It is inevitable: indeed it is right that we should thus react, for human nature is the great "I can't".

The only wrong can be if, constrained by the inner compulsions of the Spirit to this or that act of service or witness or sacrifice, we pass on from "I can't" to "I won't". If we do that, we are not merely walking *in* the flesh (normal human nature), but *after* the flesh. We shall be allying ourselves to the weakness of the flesh instead of to the power of the indwelling Spirit: and the moment we do that, we are temporarily enslaved again to the sinfulness of the flesh: natural weakness and fear then become dominated by sinful unwillingness and disobedience. Instances like Moses and Gideon show us the human responding to God's call by its natural recoil of "Who am I?" "I can't", "I am the least in my father's house". But

in neither case did the human reaction, the natural flesh,
descend to the sinful, satanic response of rebellious self—
not only, "I can't", but "I won't"; although Moses came
near to it when he said, "Lord, send someone else", and
God was angry with him.

How then, in all calls to service, do we avoid the pitfalls
of descent to rebellious flesh, and remain on the uplands
of the Spirit? Once again by participation in what Paul
calls the "bearing about in the body the dying of the Lord
Jesus, that the life also of Jesus might be made manifest
in our bodies". It is the death of Christ and His resurrection operative in service. The cross for the new man,
not the old. The cross which Jesus said must be taken up
daily, denying self, if we are to be fruit-bearers as our
Master. The cross implicit in those words, "Whosoever
will save his life shall lose it: and whosoever will lose his
life for My sake will find it."

But we must be careful here, for it is very easy to step
from grace in salvation and sanctification to works and
self-effort in service and regard service as something we
do in the way of self-sacrifice, self dedication, a giving and
expending ourselves for the world. It is this, if the true
basis is understood: if not, it becomes painful and barren
self-effort.

Paul speaks of "always bearing about in the body the
dying of *the Lord Jesus*". That is not my dying. "That the
life also of Jesus might be made manifest in our mortal
flesh." That is not my life. We still, in service, as in salvation and sanctification, know only one Saviour, Sanctifier,
Doer of all saving deeds in the world. Service is based on
what we may call a third principle of death and resurrection in action; but it is still His, not ours, or only ours by
the identification of faith.

The first work of the cross was His alone, the shedding

of His blood for the remission of sins, and the acceptance of the blood atonement as the propitiation for the world by Him who both provided a Lamb, bruised Him for our sakes, and raised Him again for our justification. It was the blood sacrifice offered unto God.

The second work of the cross was shared with us. It was the body of Jesus broken for us, crucified, dead, buried and risen, that we might be one bread and one body with Him, broken by repentance, crucified by faith, dead unto sin, buried and raised to newness of life in Him.

The third work of the cross is the dying-rising life He lives in and with and by us in our priesthood ministry for the world. It is the only way by which humanity, separated from God by the fall, can experience the resurrection life of Deity in and through it—by death in the flesh. "Put to death in the flesh, but quickened by the Spirit" is a law. Jesus Himself, the perfect human, had to die in His humanity all the days of His human life, that the life of His Father might be manifested in and through Him. He died when He returned and was subject to His parents at twelve years of age. He died when He refused those solicitations of Satan on the Mount of Temptation. He died daily as He lived the life of self-denial and took up His daily cross long before He hung on the cross of Calvary: when He did not have where to lay His head, when He was thirsty and weary, when He fed five thousand in what was meant to be a rest-period, when He bore with His disciples, when He endured the contradiction of sinners, when virtue and wisdom, not His own, flowed from Him.

The passage already referred to in 2 Cor. 4: 7-14 is Paul's clearest definition of this principle; to which we can add such references as Col. 1: 24, "filling up that which is behind of the afflictions of Christ for His body's sake";

John 12: 42, "Except a corn of wheat fall into the ground and die, it abideth alone: but if it die, it bringeth forth much fruit"; and much of the letter to the Hebrews in its earlier chapters on the human life of our great High Priest. It is the key to the triumphant ministry which Paul reveals so plainly in his Second Corinthian letter to be shot through with the cross, yet enveloped in glory. Trouble, perplexity, persecution, frustration, he calls "always bearing about in the body the dying of the Lord Jesus". Why? Because nature, flesh, must yield itself up and die to its own reactions. It is the dying of the Lord Jesus, because it is He who, living in Paul and us, deliberately takes us into adverse circumstances that He may share with us in spirit his own continuous dying to flesh-reactions. We die as we recognize ourselves as dead with Him to our own ways, praise Him, and count our adversities "all joy". Immediately we do that, the risen, ascended Christ is free in us to express Himself in His peace, love, power, guidance, and concrete actions. The dying, therefore, has been the prerequisite to the rising, "*that* the life also of Jesus might be made manifest in our mortal flesh". Our attitudes, countenances, words and deeds, then radiate the reigning Christ. No man lives unto himself, and when the human life is watered by the inner well of the abundant life, it reproduces its kind in others: "So then death worketh in us, but life in you."

The daily cross, therefore, is not, as so often presented, a grim and unwilling endurance of adversities. It is the sole principle of fruitfulness, the law of the harvest. It is not the cross for sanctification, nor the efficacy of the blood for daily cleansing. It is the continual transmuting of weak human flesh and shrinking human reactions into co-operating channels of the Spirit. We *must* die all the time, "*always* bearing about the dying of the Lord Jesus".

By no other means can weak, separated selves, confronted by all kinds of overwhelming situations, be the soil for the spiritual harvest. The supernatural life only manifests itself through the yielded natural life, and the yielding is identification with Christ in His daily dying in us. Then, Paul says, we are "perplexed, but not in despair", knocked down but not knocked out: for in our inner man rises the spirit of faith (2 Cor. 4: 13), the recognition of our identification also with an ascended Christ, seated with Him on His royal throne, victors with Him far above all opposition, and dispensers, by the authority of faith, of His gifts to men.

It means action, for no life is so dynamic, so vitalized as a Spirit-filled life. He who created, upholds and consummates all the activities of the universe, the unmoved Mover, has made us His body. A person does not have a body to feed, clothe and cleanse. Those are incidentals. A body is to use, and to use at full stretch. Is it not obvious that He who is love and who gave His only Son for the world, will likewise give us, His sons by grace? He that spared not His own Son, will He spare us? He who said, "I must work the works of Him who sent Me while it is day", will He work any the less urgently through His newly-acquired body? Nobody works like a Spirit-filled disciple. Every fibre of his being cries out, "To me to live is Christ", therefore, "I am debtor" to all the world. The zeal of God's house consumes him. The world can only go a certain distance, for it works from a centre of unrest and insufficiency: the servant of God has no limits, for his centre is the rest of faith, the endless resources of God.

Nor is there an ounce of passivity in him. "My Father still works, and I work", said Jesus, "workers together with God." God does His work by *our* minds, *our* hearts, *our* words and deeds. He sets us in action. Certainly it is dying and rising action, as we have seen. It starts by saying no to independent self-reactions, self-activities, self-inhibitions. It dies with Christ to them. But in the risen life we are altogether active. It is *our* travail, *our* sacrifice, *our* obediences of faith, *our* labours, *our* witness: yet it is really His. The paradox is true. "It all depends on God: it all depends on me." We *go* in the strength of the Lord God. It is never easy, and never will be, in the sense that there are always the steps of obedience we must take against feelings, against appearances, against natural reactions, against the tide. To that extent there is a preliminary step *we* take: at least it appears so, though actually even that is the constraint of the Spirit. That is the daily death which leads to resurrection. "Launch out into the deep . . . at Thy word I will."

Of the things which we have spoken (to quote the writer to the Hebrews), this is the sum: Not God first, but God only.